PARIS ENVIRONS

Selected points of interest discussed in this guide are printed in capital letters. Mileages between stars appear in red.

P9-AFE-593

LIFE GUIDE TO
PARIS

by The Editors of LIFE

TIME INCORPORATED

Published in association with

AMERICAN EXPRESS

New York

TIME INC. BOOK DIVISION

Editor	NORMAN P. ROSS
Copy Director	WILLIAM JAY GOLD
Art Director	EDWARD A. HAMILTON
Chief of Research	BEATRICE T. DOBIE

Editorial staff for ''LIFE Guide to Paris'':

Editor	BYRON DOBELL
Designer	CHARLES TUDOR *Assistant,* RICHARD FORTE
Copy Editor	HAROLD C. FIELD
Writers	JOHN STANTON, *Senior Writer*
	DALE M. BROWN, ANNE CHAMBERLIN, GERALD SIMONS,
	DAVID THOMSON, THOMAS WHEELER
Chief Researcher	CARLOTTA KERWIN
Researchers	BARBARA BALLANTINE, AUDREY FOOTE, NATHALIE LAGUERRE,
	DEECE LESSER, BARBARA MOIR, MADELEINE RICHARDS,
	HENRIETTE ROOSENBURG, KATHARINE SACHS, PAUL W. SCHWARTZ,
	JUDITH B. SHAW, VICTORIA STEBBINS
Picture Researchers	MARGARET K. GOLDSMITH, JOAN T. LYNCH
Art Associate	ROBERT L. YOUNG *Art Assistants,* JAMES D. SMITH, MARC RATLIFF
Cartographer	LOTHAR ROTH
Copy Staff	MARIAN GORDON GOLDMAN, CAROL HENDERSON,
	CLARICE GARRISON, DOLORES A. LITTLES

Publisher	JEROME S. HARDY
General Manager	JOHN A. WATTERS

LIFE MAGAZINE

Editor	EDWARD K. THOMPSON
Managing Editor	GEORGE P. HUNT
Publisher	C. D. JACKSON

The following individuals and departments of Time Incorporated helped in producing this book: Israel Shenker, Curtis Prendergast and other members of the Paris Bureau; Donald Bermingham of the Foreign News Service; Doris O'Neil, Chief of the LIFE Picture Library; and Content Peckham, Chief of the Bureau of Editorial Reference.

CONTENTS

PART I

A CITY IN LOVE WITH LIFE

Paris is a shrine of history, art, religion—and pleasure

A few cities are larger than Paris. Two or three capitals in Asia and in Europe are more ancient. But Paris remains the mecca of every traveler.

History never stood still in Paris. It is still being enacted today, but it does not overwhelm this city. New painting, new music, new films, new tides of taste in clothes, new philosophical movements, the boldest literature in Europe and quests for new pleasures originate there. The city of museums, of cemeteries, of libraries, of ancient religious shrines is rich in contrasts. It loves life and it turns eagerly toward the future. Its every message is one of enjoyment of the finest in peace and in life while those boons are with us. This is the most thoroughly humanized of all capitals.

Paris, the French often repeat, is not France. Yet no other French city dares rival Paris. The whole of France has deprived itself to make Paris into its brain, its heart, a harmony made of contrasts, a crucible where the metals from all the French provinces, and even from other lands, are transmuted into gold. Paris is the political and administrative capital of France, its chief industrial center, the hub of its railroads, its road and canal network, its aviation center, the cradle of literary, theatrical and artistic life. It is also the metropolis of the art of eating and of an unequaled galaxy of cafés, bars and bistros. And it is, of course, "a woman's town, with flowers in her hair."

Tourists, business travelers, women on a buying spree, students, the smart set and the unsophisticated, the hurried ones and the nonchalant ones, the old and the young visit Paris for the most varied purposes. But all of them should find in this guide what they need.

The maps and the pictures given here will bring to life the historical growth of Paris. This guidebook emphasizes that the people who created art and made history in Paris were once alive, ate, bought, loved just as their descendants do today. Behind its unity, more harmonious than that of any other metropolis, Paris conceals a never-ending and always picturesque variety of byways, recesses, markets and fairs where the people can be watched shopping, joking, flirting, quarreling, always living with zest and individuality. This guide should afford some insight into the lives of the people, rich and poor, statesmen, café waiters, taxi drivers, models, watchful *concierges* (like the one at right);

in doing so it should help provide one of the benefits of travel, an explanation of what makes other people tick so that we can be tolerantly amused at the differences between us.

Tourists do not go to Paris merely to study architecture, history and the streets and avenues of the city. They also want to buy clothes, jewels, perfumes, antiques, souvenirs. They want no less eagerly to know about restaurants, the celebrated ones where tourists discover what a refined pleasure eating can be, and some of the more modest and no less exquisite ones, dear to connoisseurs.

The French, not having gone through our own form of Puritanism, attach no unvirtuous connotation to the word "pleasure." Their restraint in the midst of enjoyment is proverbial and they hold fast to the belief that life should be rich and artistic and that Paris is the ideal shrine for such a life. With this guide, the Editors of LIFE hope to make your stay there easier, more enjoyable, more fruitful.

—HENRI M. PEYRE

Chairman
Department of Romance Languages
Yale University

THE EVOLUTION
OF A GREAT METROPOLIS

The growth of Paris to a 41-square-mile metropolis is shown on these maps of its old fortifications. For its Celtic founders, a tiny island in the Seine was fortress enough. After the conquest by Julius Caesar in 52 B.C., new ramparts dated each era of expansion. Their rise and fall has, until this century, been the sure measure of the fortunes of Paris' rulers.

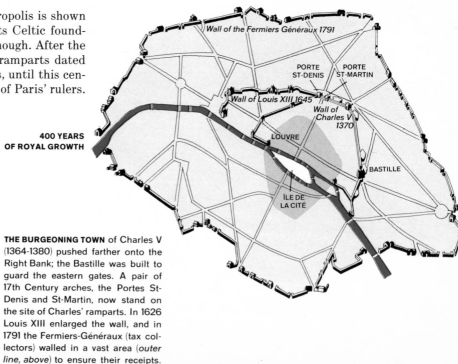

**PARIS OF
THE MIDDLE AGES**

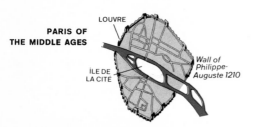

LOUVRE

ÎLE DE
LA CITÉ

Wall of
Philippe-
Auguste 1210

**400 YEARS
OF ROYAL GROWTH**

Wall of the Fermiers Généraux 1791

PORTE
ST-DENIS

PORTE
ST-MARTIN

Wall of Louis XIII 1645

Wall of
Charles V
1370

LOUVRE

BASTILLE

ÎLE DE
LA CITÉ

THE ISLAND CORE on which Paris was founded (*shown in white, above*) was the seat of temporal and spiritual authority by 1180. The north, or right, bank was becoming a major trading center; the newly founded university dominated the south, or left, bank. King Philippe-Auguste (1180-1223) encircled his prosperous city with a fortified wall and built the tower of the Louvre to protect the western side.

THE BURGEONING TOWN of Charles V (1364-1380) pushed farther onto the Right Bank; the Bastille was built to guard the eastern gates. A pair of 17th Century arches, the Portes St-Denis and St-Martin, now stand on the site of Charles' ramparts. In 1626 Louis XIII enlarged the wall, and in 1791 the Fermiers-Généraux (tax collectors) walled in a vast area (*outer line, above*) to ensure their receipts.

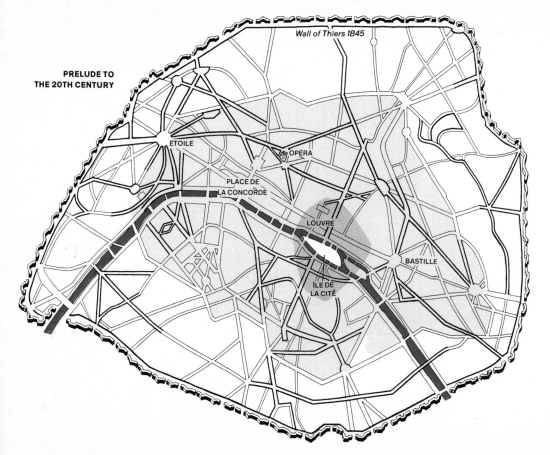

**PRELUDE TO
THE 20TH CENTURY**

Wall of Thiers 1845

ETOILE

OPÉRA

PLACE DE
LA CONCORDE

LOUVRE

BASTILLE

ÎLE DE
LA CITÉ

THE EXPANDED CITY, now bursting with 19 centuries of treasure, with lovely jewels of Gothic architecture and Renaissance masterpieces, with parks and squares and magnificent homes, was enclosed for the last time in 1845. The fortifications of Premier Alphonse Thiers (*outer line at left*) almost outline the cup-of-champagne shape of today's Paris. By 1870 the vigorous Baron Haussmann had driven his grand boulevards through the maze of medieval streets. His broad avenues (emphasized by darker lines on the map) were built partly to allow government troops freedom to maneuver in the strife-haunted Paris of Napoleon III (1852-1870).

The last walls were razed in 1919; they have been replaced by circular highways. With a 7.8 million population in its metropolitan area, Paris has now expanded beyond the natural boundaries of its encircling hills. As the Seine passes through this metropolis it makes a great loop, first north, then south. Then the river continues very slowly to the sea, as if in reluctance to leave Paris behind.

EMINENT MEN WHO SHAPED PARIS' HISTORY

In the age of faith:
a holy king

From an audacious Renaissance

From Revolution and Empire

From the Second Empire

Proud of the great men who have been born or come to live within its walls, Paris has memorialized them in the names of its boulevards, its bridges and even its Métro stops. Those whose luster is greatest are immortalized on postage stamps like the ones shown here, miniature recordings of heroes and history.

Louis IX, later St Louis (*above*), reigned in the 13th Century, in the great age of Gothic cathedrals. He sponsored the Sorbonne and built Sainte-Chapelle (*pages 40-43*); both survive. He was canonized for his good works.

Paris plunged into the excitement of the Renaissance with Henri IV (*top row, first stamp*), who unified the kingdom of France. Forced to convert to Catholicism in order to ascend the throne, he cynically joked that "Paris is well worth a mass." As the Renaissance matured, La Fontaine wrote his prudent but delightful fables; Molière established his great theatrical company, which became the Comédie

8

to the Age of Romanticism

to the discovery of radium

Française and Pascal wrote his celebrated *Pensées*, which aimed at converting unbelievers. A patron of the arts, Cardinal Richelieu, the King's ruthless First Minister, built within the Palais-Royal the most artistic and serene garden in Paris (*pages 106-107*). Under the Sun King, Louis XIV, French manners, language and art were supreme in Europe. He built the Place des Victoires, with its equestrian statue, and the Place Vendôme (*pages 134-135*).

Voltaire (*middle row, first stamp*) was a fighter against oppression who laid the philosophical groundwork for the French Revolution. Many of its leaders, like Robespierre and Danton, came from the provinces but perished on the guillotine in the city's heart. Out of the revolution's flames came Napoleon. As emperor he built the Rue de Rivoli, the Rue de la Paix, the Madeleine and the Arc de Triomphe. He admired Madame Récamier, who attracted great men with her beauty and wit. In these years the tumultuous Romantic era erupted, typified by the painter Delacroix.

Conservative virtues of 19th Century France are epitomized in the Emperor Louis Napoleon (*bottom row, first stamp*). He appointed Baron Haussmann to be his great builder. No man did more to create the Paris of today. It was an age of progress: Niepce invented and Daguerre developed the art of photography. It was an age of despair, reflected in the symbolist poetry of Baudelaire. Its close saw mankind step onto the threshold of a new world. On December 26, 1898, Madame Curie, working with her husband Pierre, announced their discovery of radium. Their research in radioactivity led to today's atomic revolution.

AN INTERNATIONAL AFFAIR OF THE HEART

For Americans, Paris abounds in reminders of the long and cordial association of the U.S. and France, beginning with the American Revolution, which French arms helped to win. And over the years Americans who came to Paris—to fight or write or simply visit—found there a second home.

AN ASTUTE ENVOY, Benjamin Franklin (*left*) is crowned by Liberty in a 1779 etching by a French admirer. In Paris, he won France's heart and persuaded it to aid America. A bust of Franklin is in the Louvre; the Rue Franklin is off the Place du Trocadéro.

LIBERTY, symbol of Franco-American friendship, towers outlandishly above her Paris workshop before being sent to New York harbor in 1885. Money from the French people built the statue as a gift commemorating joint efforts in the American Revolution.

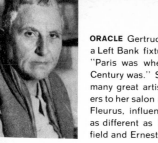

ORACLE Gertrude Stein was a Left Bank fixture to whom "Paris was where the 20th Century was." She attracted many great artists and writers to her salon at 27 Rue de Fleurus, influenced authors as different as Louis Bromfield and Ernest Hemingway.

NOVELIST Ernest Hemingway worked as a reporter in Paris after World War I. His favorite cafés were the Dôme and the Select on the Boulevard Montparnasse. In the picture he wears a bandage for head wounds he suffered during a bohemian Left Bank party.

PRODIGAL F. Scott Fitzgerald fled from the harassments of New York for the Right Bank, the Ritz Hotel bar and the Riviera. For him France was a wild party; for Left Bank expatriates it was an intellectual banquet served up at a favorable rate of exchange.

A PARIS THRONG welcomes Charles Lindbergh's plane on May 21, 1927. His nonstop flight from New York, which won a prize offered to strengthen ties with France, was made in 33½ hours. He landed at Le Bourget, still in use today as a Paris airport

LES YANKS, the second successive generation to fight in France, parade along the Champs-Élysées after helping free Paris in 1944. Many returned as students and as businessmen, inspiring novel ventures for Paris such as milk bars and supermarkets.

11

PART II

A PARIS PRIMER

Here are the answers to a tourist's questions

What is the best time to see Paris? Any time. Best of the best is between the blossoming of the chestnut trees in April and the day they celebrate the fall of the Bastille on July 14 with parades, fireworks on Montmartre and the banks of the Seine, and dancing in the streets. But Paris is soft and luminous in autumn, languorous in August and glowing at Christmas. The calendar of events (*page 156*) will help you plan.

What weather can you expect? Paris is cooler in summer and less frigid in winter than most northern U.S. cities. The table just below indicates the average temperature range.

TEMP.	JAN.	FEB.	MARCH	APRIL	MAY	JUNE	JULY	AUG.	SEPT.	OCT.	NOV.	DEC.
Low	35	39	41	45	49	55	58	57	55	47	41	37
High	44	50	55	60	67	71	75	73	70	61	50	46
Aver.	39.5	44.5	48	52.5	58	63	65.5	65	62.5	54	45.5	41.5

You can expect rain just a shade under 50 per cent of the time

What is the first thing to do? Either through your travel agent or on your own, send ahead for hotel reservations; the city is often crowded. (For hotel information, see page 158.)

What clothes should you take? Dress conservatively as you would in any large U.S. city. Regardless of the season, there are two essentials—a raincoat (preferably one that can double as an after-dark coat) and comfortable walking shoes. In summer loud sports shirts for men are out; so are women's slacks, shorts and beach dresses. Jackets are worn by men except in more modest restaurants. Most useful for a woman is a gay, décolleté print dress with matching jacket which can be worn or not as the occasion demands. In winter you will be more comfortable if you dress more warmly indoors than you do at home—take a sweater, stole or small fur. A dark suit is appropriate for a man on most occasions, a basic dark dress a must for a woman. Formal clothes are not necessary but can come in handy for gala occasions.

What else should you take? Take soap, for you will not find it everywhere. Take cigarettes; you can bring in 1,000 of them, and French tobacco takes getting used to. If you wear glasses, bring a spare set plus the prescription. Bring spare false teeth. French customs will let you bring in at least one of just about anything—and binoculars are useful.

What about taking pictures? The French positively encourage it. You have the right to bring in two still cameras (provided they are of different makes) and one movie camera. To avoid trouble with U.S. customs on your return, get a U.S. receipt for the new camera you take along or register it with U.S. customs before leaving. For each still camera, you can bring in 10 rolls of film or 12 plates, and for the movie camera, 10 rolls. Remember, film costs a lot in France.

How will you be received? No matter how you arrive, by ship or by air, you'll find customs officers are understanding men who mostly make chalk marks on your baggage and smile you on. After customs at airfields, taxicabs will offer to take you into town, but this will cost 12-15 NF ($2.40-$3.00) as against 3 NF (60 cents) by bus. However, late at night, buses do not run often. At the air terminal (Aérogare des Invalides) there are "Paris Hostesses," English-speaking women who will find you a taxi and direct you to your hotel. The same is true at St-Lazare station, where Le Havre and Cherbourg boat trains arrive. Travelers reaching the city via southern or northern Europe will also get this service.

Will you like the French? Nowadays the spirited, bubbly Frenchman, as created by Maurice Chevalier, is hard to find in France itself. The real Frenchman can be somewhat cold and reserved. This is because the Frenchman is serious. To him, thrift is a beautiful quality; the seeming affluence of the tourists may be disconcerting. Traditionally the Frenchman is insular; he is convinced Paris is the center of the world. This can be provoking. But with an understanding heart, and a willingness to meet them halfway, you will find the French can be agreeable and witty.

What is special in Paris? The coffee, roasted black, is very strong. Young people clutch and kiss even as they walk briskly to work. Everybody shakes hands even if it holds up traffic to do so, and a French gentleman kisses a married lady's hand in greeting her. Lunch can last for two hours and afterward traffic moves faster for the litre of good wine drivers have washed their meal down with. If you go to a restaurant for dinner at 6 p.m. you will be alone, for the Paris dinner hour begins at 8 p.m. The cafés usually take pari-mutuel bets on the races; many Frenchmen place a bet every day.

THE FINANCIAL FACTS:
HOW TO COPE WITH THEM

How expensive is it? Paris is about as expensive as New York, Chicago or Los Angeles. On a fixed-price tour, the overall costs are set in advance, but budget-busting temptations abound on all sides. The visitor on his own will find prices higher because he wants to live in style. Double rooms in luxury hotels cost $15 a day and up, and an evening at a famous restaurant can cost $40 a person or more. Double rooms can be had in less luxurious hotels for $10 a night (*pages 158-161*). Hundreds of restaurants offer superb meals at prices ranging from $5 to $7 for lunch for two and $10 to $12 for dinner (*pages 162-173*); yet a tourist can live student-style on the Left Bank for $5 a day. But Paris is a glittery place and most people are willing to pay to see it properly.

How should I buy francs? Before leaving the U.S. buy $10 worth of francs at any bank. Use this for tips and taxis on your arrival in Paris. Keep the rest of your money in traveler's checks. Many hotels, the majority of restaurants and all French banks will cash your traveler's checks; so will the exchange offices at the airfields and railroad stations,

American and British travel agencies, and banks scattered all over town. The rates vary only by pennies per $100; there is no longer a black market, and you won't be cheated.

How is French money figured? This looks more complicated than it is. The only possible source of confusion is the fact that France, in 1960, issued New Francs (NF), but the old francs are also still in circulation. One NF (20 cents) is the equivalent of 100 old francs (also worth 20 cents); there was no devaluation, merely a change in numbering scheme. About 70 per cent of the bills in circulation are NF, or New Francs. The rest are old francs, marked simply francs (strike the last two digits and you know their worth in NF); and "transition" francs, which have both the old and the new denominations printed on them. Also being circulated are NF coins and their old-franc equivalents (100 centimes make a franc): the 5 NF coin and 500 old-franc banknote, 1 NF and 100 old-franc coins, 50 new-centime and 50 old-franc coins; 20 new-centime and 20 old-franc coins, 10 new-centime and 10 old-franc coins as well as some even smaller change.

New Francs vs. Dollars	
NF	$
.50	.10
1	.20
5	1.00
7.50	1.50
10	2.00
50	10.00
100	20.00
500	100.00

ONE NEW FRANC EQUALS 100 OLD FRANCS

How much to tip? Many Europeans argue that Americans tip so generously that they spoil those who are providing the services. Pay no attention to this argument. Tipping generates good service, and service is what you want. In Paris, as in large U.S. cities, 12 to 15 per cent of a bill is considered a reasonable tip. One important difference: most French hotels and restaurants add the tip to the bill. The charge is called *service* and the revenue from it is divided among the staff. If *service* is included, a token tip of loose change (1 NF or less) is customary—not so much as a tip but as a personal "thank you," a gesture in appreciation of good service. To help you distinguish between the good tip and the ostentatious tip, here are some suggestions:

RAILROAD PORTER	He has a fixed fee: 70 centimes per piece of luggage. One NF a bag will amply cover his fee and the tip.
HOTEL BAGGAGE PORTER	He is usually tipped 1 NF a bag unless there are more than three. Then he gets less: 50 centimes each.
CHAMBERMAID	She is covered by the service charge but should get 3 to 5 NF a week for special services like pressing.
VALET SERVICE	This service is also accounted for in the hotel bill. Anything extra you give is for extra services required.
CAFÉ OR RESTAURANT CHECKROOM	To rescue a man's hat and coat costs 50 centimes to 1 NF depending on how luxurious the establishment is.
BARTENDER	French barmen expect from 12 to 15 per cent of the bill, so tip them if service is not included in the charge.
TABLE WAITER	In most French restaurants service is included in the bill. Leave loose change anyway. But if menu says

Service non compris, you should tip from 12 to 20 per cent, depending on the luxuriousness of the restaurant.

HEADWAITER	Headwaiters are tipped only in de luxe restaurants for de luxe service. For the others, a smile is enough.
WINE STEWARD	The steward, called *sommelier*, is not covered by *service*. Tip him at least 1 NF; more at top restaurants.
WASHROOM ATTENDANT	The normal tip in this case is 50 centimes, but when you buy cigarettes or other items the tip goes up.
THEATER CHECKROOM	The prices, usually 50 centimes an item, are posted on the wall. But loose change is also welcome here.
THEATER USHER	For seating two people: a tip of 50 centimes to 1 NF.
PROGRAM VENDOR	Give 20 centimes more than the price of the program.
MOVIE USHER	For seating two people a tip of 50 centimes is fine.
BARBER AND HAIRDRESSER	In barber and beauty shops the service charge sometimes is included in the total; if not, tip 15 per cent.
MUSEUM GUIDE	For an extended tour the guide expects a tip of at least 50 centimes from each member of a large group.
TOUR CONDUCTOR	Bus tour conductors count on tips. If you tip 15 per cent of the cost of your ticket they will be quite happy.
TELEPHONE OPERATOR	If she has been interpreting for you on the phone, or making complicated calls, give her up to 2 NF per call.
DOORMAN	For hailing a taxi a doorman expects a tip of 50 centimes; if it is raining, then a tip of 1 NF is in order.
HOTEL CONCIERGE	A tip of 5 to 10 NF per week in average-priced hotels; 20 to 30 NF in an expensive hotel if the services have been numerous, less for fewer, nothing for none. If he or his assistants has executed more complicated tasks, like buying pills at 2 a.m., more is expected.

SIX PARISIANS YOU NEED
ON YOUR SIDE

When you arrive in Paris you will discover that certain key Parisians control your destiny, and there is something particularly Parisian in the way each one goes about it.

Your station or airport *porteur* (porter) will be your first encounter with Parisian life. (See page 15 for details on tipping for services in Paris.)

L'agent (the Paris policeman) if treated with respect will help you when you are lost. *Le chauffeur de taxi* (taxi driver) will take you where you're going if you can pronounce the address or show it to him in this guide. If anything happens to your *concierge*, leave France.

You can linger almost indefinitely at your sidewalk table over a *café filtre* (strong black coffee) without arousing so much as an unkind look from *le garçon* (café waiter). He will also get you a more filling snack if you want it.

On a visit to either the movies or the live theater you will meet *l'ouvreuse* (the usherette) who, unlike American ushers, expects to be tipped for seating you. However, neither she nor anyone else can protect you from ferocious mutterings should you arrive late and take too long getting settled.

LE PORTEUR wears the blue overblouse, with an identifying number on the front, that shows him to be a porter. At train stations like the Gare St-Lazare, where you might meet Jean Cantero (*above*), hand him your bags out the window. At airports the porter will find you. Remember his number, meet him at the taxi stand. He won't lose a thing.

L'AGENT, a Paris cop like José Germa (*above*), spends an exasperating and very risky day amid the chaos and anarchy of one of the world's wildest traffic patterns. If you make a wrong turn or walk against traffic, you may find him a bit testy. But addressed respectfully as *Monsieur l'Agent*, he will help you and, in central Paris, he may speak English.

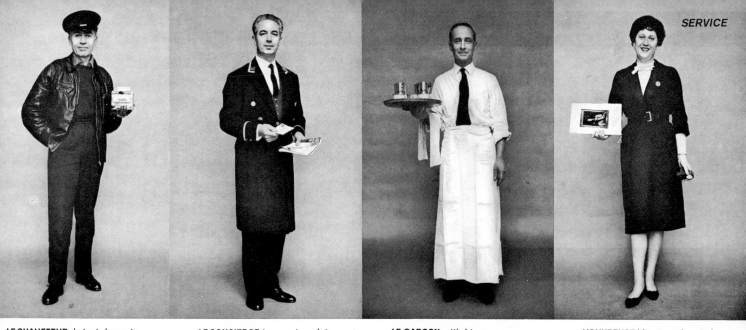

LE CHAUFFEUR de taxi shown is Wladimir Netchaeff, one of the legendary White Russians. He owns his own cab, an old six-passenger Citroën, and writes poetry in his spare time. Not all drivers are poets, so it helps to write down the address. But if the destination conflicts with a driver's inclination, he may ignore it or plead poor eyes as an excuse to avoid taking you.

LE CONCIERGE is an untranslatable term for the irreplaceable man who, like Joseph Lando of the Hôtel Lotti (*above*), is receptionist, bell captain, money-changer, message taker (so be sure he knows how your name is pronounced) and your single most important ally in Paris. He hires cars, arranges tours, gets tickets, can rent dinner jackets or get your aching teeth pulled.

LE GARÇON with his ever-present metal coffee pot will soon become a familiar and helpful figure to you if you follow the Parisians' habits of newspaper-reading, letter-writing or people-watching at their sidewalk cafés. Like many experienced café waiters, Max Keck (*above*) of the Café Bar de l'Ambassade prides himself on his grasp of English food and drink terms.

L'OUVREUSE (theater usherette) named Claire Delavault is in her 18th year of showing people to their seats at the Comédie Française. Naturally she knows all the details of the theater's programs and the seating plan by heart. She likes Tuesday evenings best because they are formal. Be sure your change is ready as you are being seated to avoid fumbling in the dark.

17

HOW TO KEEP
IN TOUCH

What about public telephones? Dial the first three letters of an exchange, plus two sets of double figures—thus OBS 85-29. Public phones take *jetons,* or tokens (*below*). Cost: 37 centimes for the small *jeton* in post office and *Métro* phones and 50 centimes for the larger one good in restaurants. After someone answers push the button "A" and talk. If no one answers and button "A" isn't pushed, your *jeton* is returned. At post offices, operators will place your call.

PUBLIC TELEPHONE
BOOTH "JETON"

RESTAURANT OR
CAFÉ "JETON"

How much to call home? Charges are 59.25 NF ($11.85) for three minutes and 19.75 ($3.95) for each extra minute. Person-to-person adds 3.71 NF (75 cents) per call. There are English-speaking operators manning the overseas lines.

What about cables? They cost from 1.36 to 1.75 NF per word to the U.S. Send them through your hotel *concierge.* Or do it yourself at the nearest post office. There is all-night service at 8 Place de la Bourse (*map, pages 126-127, X-7*) and 103 Rue de Grenelle (*map, pages 88-89, T-5*).

What about the time differential? This is of great importance in making telephone calls and sending cables home. If you call at 9 a.m., the call will reach home at 3 a.m. Paris is six hours ahead of Eastern Standard Time and you must remember to make additional adjustments for daylight saving time and for the time zone of your home town.

Special delivery? The *pneumatique* service in Paris and its suburbs accepts ordinary letter paper up to 9 p.m. Or you can get a *petit bleu,* a small blue form on which to write your message. This moves by pneumatic tube in about two hours and costs from 1.25 NF to 2 NF, depending on weight.

How to mail letters back home? The simplest way is to give the letters to the *concierge.* But there are mail boxes, painted blue, all around. Stamps can be bought not only in the post offices but also in tobacco stores and from the *concierge,* and there is no reason why you should not mail your own letters. This way you can be certain that your airmail letters are going by airmail. Rates from France to the U.S. are: post cards, 30 centimes; airmail post cards, 65 centimes; letters (one ounce), 50 centimes; airmail letters (one sheet), 85 centimes; and letters inside France, 25 centimes.

Emergency Addresses They are useful though few need them. But when you do you really do and so, here they are:

GENERAL EMERGENCIES

American Embassy
2 Avenue Gabriel
(ANJ 74-60)

Préfecture de Police
7 Boulevard du Palais
(DAN 44-20)

American Aid Society
49 Rue Pierre-Charron
(BAL 66-49)

MEDICAL EMERGENCIES

The American Hospital of Paris
63 Boulevard Victor-Hugo
Neuilly-sur-Seine
(MAI 68-00)

(Note: If you need a dentist,
consult the American Hospital.)

British and American Pharmacy
1 Rue Auber
(OPE 49-40)

Guenot Pharmacy
(Open until 12:30 a.m.)
14 Avenue Mozart
(JAS 38-17)

Le Drug Store des Champs-Élysées
133 Avenue des Champs-Élysées
(BAL 94-40)

(Note: There is one drugstore open in
every neighborhood at all times every
day. The list of open stores is posted
on the doors of all. And police can
also guide you to an open pharmacy.)

LOST OBJECTS

Service des Objets Trouvés
36 Rue des Morillons
(No telephone queries answered.)

(Note: The service charges a
flat fee of 1.50 NF on all articles found
regardless of value. Though not
obligatory, one may give an additional
10 per cent of value of article.)

LOST OR SICK ANIMALS

La Fourrière (The Pound)
39 Rue de Dantzig
(BLO 81-00)

Veterinary School Clinic
33 Rue de Citeaux
(DID 17-13)

Useful French Words and Phrases

If you have no French at all, no list of commonly used words can give you any feeling of ease. But what follows will help you read signs and ask for assistance. Don't attempt to pronounce; point to the relevant words.

NUMBERS one, *un*; two, *deux*; three, *trois*; four, *quatre*; five, *cinq*; six, *six*; seven, *sept*; eight, *huit*; nine, *neuf*; ten, *dix*; twenty, *vingt*; thirty, *trente*; forty, *quarante*; fifty, *cinquante*; one hundred, *cent*; one thousand, *mille*.

THE DAYS OF THE WEEK Monday, *lundi*; Tuesday, *mardi*; Wednesday, *mercredi*; Thursday, *jeudi*; Friday, *vendredi*; Saturday, *samedi*; Sunday, *dimanche*.

SIGNS no smoking, *défense de fumer*; go slow, *ralentir*; no admittance, *défense d'entrer*; entrance, *entrée*; exit, *sortie*; ladies, *dames*; gentlemen, *messieurs*; information, *renseignements*; keep off the grass, *défense de marcher sur le gazon*; one-way street, *sens unique*; free, *libre*; forbidden, *interdit*; caution, *attention*.

CABLES AND MAIL Where is the cable office? *Où est le bureau des cables?* I want to send this package. *Je voudrais envoyer ce paquet.* I want it insured. *Je voudrais l'assurer.* Please give me ten airmail stamps for the United States. *Donnez-moi dix timbres par avion pour les États-Unis, s'il vous plait.*

DIRECTIONS right, *à droit*; left, *à gauche*; straight ahead, *tout droit*; up, *en haut*; down, *en bas*; stop, *arrêtez*; go ahead, *continuez*; hurry, *dépêchez-vous*; street, *rue*; avenue, *avenue*.

EMERGENCIES I've been robbed! *On m'a volé!* I have lost my baggage. *J'ai perdu mes bagages.* I have lost my passport. *J'ai perdu mon passeport.* Help! *Au secours!*

HOTEL FRENCH
See page 158.

RESTAURANT FRENCH
See pages 162-173.

GETTING AROUND TOWN
LIKE A PARISIAN

How does the "Métro" work? The *Métro*, or subway, is the easiest way to get around. Maps at all stations, on the platforms and in the cars (*see below*), show routes and transfer points. At about one in three stations, there is an electrical route indicator. Press the button next to your destination and your entire route, including transfer points (called *correspondances*), lights up. Paris is built on a circular street plan, so it is often necessary to change trains, but the maps and signs at all stations will keep you straight. You buy tickets at a booth one flight down from street level, and these are stamped at the entrance to the train platform. Keep your tickets to show fare inspectors. A gate prevents people from reaching the platform when a train is approaching or standing in the station. When the train arrives, lift a car door latch and slide the double doors open.

How do I find my way around? Study the front end-paper map in this book. After you have learned a few points of reference—the Seine, the Place de l'Opéra on the Right Bank, the Boulevard St-Germain on the Left Bank—the pieces will fall into place. The seven street maps in this guide, used with the directory (*pages 156-197*), do the rest.

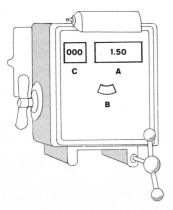

HOW ABOUT TAXIS? You may well decide to explore Paris by taxi. If so, write the address and show it to the driver. Then look at the meter, which should read 1.50 NF during the day (see window A in the drawing at left). If it reads more, you are being charged for the previous trip. After the initial 1.50 NF, it's 20 centimes for each one fourth of a mile; after 11 p.m., night rates are nearly double, but pay them only if window B shows a number two. Trunks and other heavy baggage bring on an extra charge shown in window C.

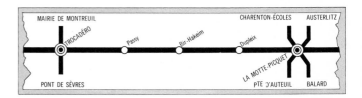

WHAT DO TICKETS COST? *Métro* tickets (*right*) are sold individually and in books of 20 called *carnets* (5.60 NF for first class and 3.70 for second). First-class cars are painted red, offer some added comfort.

Will buslines confuse you? Not necessarily. A simplified bus map appears on the back end papers of this guide. Bus stops have posts with the numbers of the buses that stop there. There is also an automatic dispenser of numbered slips of paper: take one and stand in line. When the bus comes in, the conductor will call *"priorités"* and the disabled, the blind, and pregnant women will board first. Others then board according to their numbered slips. You buy your ticket book from the conductor. The map posted in the bus (*see below*) shows the number of segments to your destination; give the conductor that number of tickets and he will stamp them. Keep your tickets in case an inspector asks to see them. Press the bell in the middle of the car or near the exit to leave the bus. Watch for street signs for your destination; the conductor's shouts are not always intelligible.

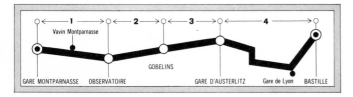

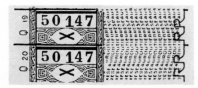

ARE BUSES COSTLY? Tickets (*left*) are 3.70 NF for a book of 20. Each is good for one segment of the line. Length of the segments (*map above*) is roughly one third of a mile.

Can you hire an automobile? Yes, you can, with or without chauffeur. If you are going to take trips outside of Paris, an automobile can be a delight and, for a family, even an economy. But inside Paris the automobile is the same annoyance it is in any large city: you are trapped in traffic; you can't find a parking place; you wish the car had wings. Rentals range from around 23 NF per day for a small Renault to 70 NF per day for an American car. This usually includes 60 kilometers; additional mileage adds to the cost. Companies renting cars include: Hertz, 43 Rue Bayen (Telephone ETO 65-75); Mattéi, 207 Rue de Bercy (DOR 75-91); and Neubauer, 11 Boulevard Gouvion-St -Cyr (ETO 75-33).

Is driving different? Your driver's license is perfectly good in France. A liter is about a quart, and four liters of gas are a gallon, and the kilometer, the European measure of distance, is five eighths of a mile. Blowing horns is forbidden except in real emergency in Paris. In traffic circles as elsewhere, cars which enter from the right have priority.

Any other way to see Paris? Yes, a most pleasant and expensive way (8 to 10 NF an hour) is by horse-drawn fiacre, or carriage. There are still a few around the Eiffel Tower, the Opéra, the Tuileries and along the Champs-Élysées; a drive through the Bois de Boulogne is worth a few extra NF.

Want a bargain? Then buy a $4.25 special seven-day first-class combined *Métro*, urban and suburban busline ticket available at the R.A.T.P. booth in the Place de la Madeleine.

HELPFUL HINTS
ON GETTING SETTLED

What about visiting? It is very unusual for the French to entertain in their homes. A Frenchman's home is very much his private castle and he much prefers to meet and entertain in a café or restaurant. It is, therefore, a rare honor to be invited to lunch or even to tea, and dinner invitations are rarer still. The best family linen, crystal, silver and china will be used, the wines will be excellent, the food elaborate. Tea parties are equally formal and will *not* merge into a relaxed cocktail hour. This formality comes in large part from the Frenchman's sense that in opening his house to an outsider he is putting his dignity, his honor and his family's honor on the line. In such circumstances punctuality is essential, and easy American bonhomie will not do. The French normally address each other as *"monsieur"* or *"madame"* and shake hands on meeting and departing. You should do the same. It is proper to take a present to your hostess, preferably a box of candy. A bottle of wine is not proper; whisky is acceptable on the fourth or fifth occasion. Unless you are a single woman traveling alone, be sure to send a bouquet of flowers with your card the next day.

Can you meet people? It is difficult to meet the French on a casual, social basis. However, there are organizations dedicated to easing the way for Americans who want to meet Frenchmen with similar interests. Some of them:

U.S. Chamber of Commerce, 21 Avenue George V (BAL 01-54)

Technical Tourism Committee, 31 Avenue Pierre-1er-de-Serbie (KLE 67-30). Arranges tours and meetings with manufacturers as a service of the Conseil National du Patronat Français, the French NAM

CEGOS (Center of Industrial Studies), 12 Rue Blaise-Pascal, Neuilly-sur-Seine (SAB 78-30). Sets up plant visits and provides industrial information

Centre National du Commerce Extérieur, 10 Avenue d'Iéna (KLE 17-90). Arranges meetings between Americans and Frenchmen engaged in foreign trade

Lions Club, 74 Avenue des Champs-Élysées (ELY 33-01)

Rotary Club, 11 bis Rue de Presbourg (POI 57-17)

Centre International du Film Médical et Chirurgical, 36 Rue de Ponthieu (BAL 73-41). Arranges for American doctors to see films of operations performed by French doctors

Association Française des Femmes Médecines, 123 Rue de Lille (INV 29-29). Arranges meetings between French and American women physicians

Comité d'Accueil du Comité de Liaison des Associations Féminines Françaises, 14 Avenue Georges-Mandel (PAS 96-60). Arranges meetings between officers of French and American women's clubs

Union Mondiale des Organizations Féminines Catholiques, 91 Rue de Sèvres (BAB 27-54). Arranges meetings between French and American Catholic clubwomen

Office du Tourism Universitaire, 137 Boulevard St-Michel (DAN 60-97). Arranges meetings with university students

Churches with English Services See page 193.

Electrical Gadgets Electrical appliances require an adapter (available in the U.S.) to fit French outlets. Always check with the *concierge* before using appliances.

Newspapers Available in the kiosks (newsstands), usually on the same day they appear at home, are overseas editions of American news magazines and continental editions of New York and London newspapers. Most useful weekly calendar of events is *Paris Weekly Information,* on sale (.50 NF) at kiosks and in hotels.

Pressing, Cleaning, Laundry Enlist the aid of the hotel.

Drinking Water It is perfectly safe.

What's Closed When Most stores are closed Sundays and Mondays. Many are closed for vacation in August.

Dogs and Cats A pet must be accompanied by a health certificate. The certificate should state it has had an antirabies vaccination or has lived for six months in an area rabies-free for three years.

Travel Agents AmericanExpress, 11 Rue Scribe (OPE 42-90), the best-known gathering place for Americans in Paris, offers travel, car rental and financial services as well as a Paris mail address. Tourist services also are provided by Thomas Cook & Son, 2 Place de la Madeleine (OPE 40-40).

More Addresses to Help You

GENERAL INFORMATION

Welcome Information Office, 7 Rue Balzac (ELY 52-78 or ELY 48-00). Questions will be answered in English by Paris Hostesses

AIRLINES

Air France, 2 Rue Scribe (OPE 41-00) or 119 Avenue des Champs-Élysées (BAL 70-50)

Pan American World Airways, 1 Rue Scribe or 138 Avenue des Champs-Élysées (BAL 88-00)

Trans World Airlines, 5 Rue Scribe or 101 Avenue des Champs-Élysées (BAL 10-83)

AUTOMOBILE ASSOCIATIONS

American Automobile Association, 9 Rue de la Paix (OPE 35-08)

Automobile Club de France, 6-8 Place de la Concorde (ANJ 34-70)

Touring Club de France, 65 Avenue de la Grande-Armée (PAS 62-65)

BOOKS IN ENGLISH

Brentano's bookstore, 37 Avenue de l'Opéra (OPE 60-04)

Galignani's bookstore, 224 Rue de Rivoli (OPE 56-98)

W. H. Smith & Son bookstore, 248 Rue de Rivoli (RIC 40-73)

The American Library, 129 Avenue des Champs-Élysées (BAL 54-89)

PAWNSHOPS

Credit Municipal (main office), 55 Rue des Francs-Bourgeois (TUR 33-29)

STEAMING AND BAKING

Turkish Bath, Hotel Claridge, 74 Avenue des Champs-Élysées (ELY 33-01)

Le Cordon Bleu, 129 Rue du Faubourg-St-Honoré (ELY 35-39). French cooking school with a one-day course

7 AN ENCHANTED FOREST

2 IMAGES OF GLORY

6 THE HEIGHTS AND THE DEPTHS

5 THE BUSTLING CENTER

4 CABBAGES AND KINGS

3 SENTINEL OF THE NATION

1 THE MIND AND THE SPIRIT

MONTMARTRE

Sacré-Coeur

Étoile

Opéra

Les Halles

RIGHT BANK

Louvre

LEFT BANK

Tour Eiffel

MARAIS

BOIS DE
BOULOGNE

Notre-Dame

MONTPARNASSE

QUARTIER
LATIN

BOIS DE
VINCENNES

THE SIGHTS of Paris are grouped under seven titles on the map above. They are described and mapped in detail on the pages which follow. High points shown in blue are for orientation.

24

PART III THE SEVEN FACES OF PARIS

What to see and why: a pattern for touring the city

Encrusted with history and bursting with life, Paris presents to the visitor a marvelous variety of faces. As a result, the unprepared tourist frequently finds his visit becoming a bewildering succession of disconnected impressions. For the pages that follow, therefore, seven dominant aspects of Paris (*map, opposite*) have been selected. They are described in a way designed to help the visitor decide what he will find most interesting in all that he encounters.

"The Mind and the Spirit" of Paris can best be understood by visits to the great religious edifices on the Île de la Cité and a walk through the intellectual center, the Latin Quarter. "Images of Glory" shine from the art of the Louvre and along the stately Champs-Élysées to the Arc de Triomphe. The Eiffel Tower, symbol of Paris as a "Sentinel of the Nation," sends its spire above a cluster of government buildings as well as the Dome of the Invalides, beneath which Napoleon and his imperial dreams lie entombed. "Cabbages and Kings" is the theme of the Marais area, with its relics of the old royalist regimes and today's central markets, which feed the city. "The Bustling Center" is the workaday and elegant mixture of downtown Paris. "The Heights and the Depths" describes the hill of Montmartre, high above a raffish night life. Finally comes "An Enchanted Forest," the hushed, remotely nearby Bois de Boulogne.

With this guide in hand, and following the detailed maps which introduce each aspect of the city, you may explore Paris in your own way. For those who like to walk—and there is no city in the world more delightful for strolling—four walking tours are included. But no matter how you travel, this part of the guide will be your good companion.

● *Bus tours: American Express, Thomas Cook & Son (pages 22-23) and other travel agencies offer a wide variety of guided tours of the city and its environs. So does the city-run RATP, next to the Madeleine. Cityrama—2 bis Rue de Juillet, RIC 43-90—has glass-domed buses that tour Paris with a dramatic running commentary, tape-recorded in eight languages. Night bus tours are listed in the Paris "Herald-Tribune," "Paris Weekly Information" and "Semaine de Paris." Boat tours: The Bateaux Mouches boats leave from Pont de l'Alma and the Vedettes Paris-Tour Eiffel boats from Pont d'Iéna (map, pages 88-89, N-1 and J-4). Prices range from 5 NF for a 1 1/2-hour cruise to 45 NF for a 2 1/2-hour trip with gourmet dinner.*

1

THE MIND AND THE SPIRIT

On the banks of the Seine are some of the greatest monuments of the western world which reveal the easy mingling of mind and spirit that has made Paris a cosmopolis. The Palais de Justice, or law courts, which sprawls near Notre-Dame, enfolds the fragile stained glass of the Sainte-Chapelle. At the same time the Palais includes the Conciergerie, an ancient prison. In the Latin Quarter stand the buildings of the university. Here Paris has molded the most serious minds of Europe for centuries. Here, too, is the Panthéon, burial place of famous Frenchmen. But close by, Montparnasse and St-Germain des Prés, scene of artists' joys and agonies, maintain the tradition of intellect and wit.

HIGHLIGHTS shown in red (*left*) are covered in detail in the following pages; other points of interest in this area appear in black.

A SILVER THREAD
RUNNING THROUGH THE CITY

The Seine River curves in a long arc through Paris from east to west for seven miles. Along its banks, as the picture at the right demonstrates so eloquently, are the great monuments of a beauty-loving civilization. From the bell tower of the Hôtel de Ville (Paris' City Hall) in the foreground to the Tour St-Jacques on the far right and down the center, over the rooftops of the Louvre to the Grand-Palais and the Arc de Triomphe—all this is elegant and historic Paris, linked together by the river's silvery thread. For most Parisians the Seine is Paris: they have bathed in it, fished in it, many years ago they washed their clothing in it, boated on it and fought in wars for it. Many can remember being flooded out of their homes by it; 1915 was the last time. But above all it is lovely, and no better way exists to savor this city than to stroll slowly along the river banks. On the pages that follow, such a walk is outlined.

A CITY OF BRIDGES, Paris has 32 of them over the Seine. In age they range from the Pont Neuf (1606), second from bottom in the picture, to the newest permanent one, the Pont du Carrousel (1939), the fourth.

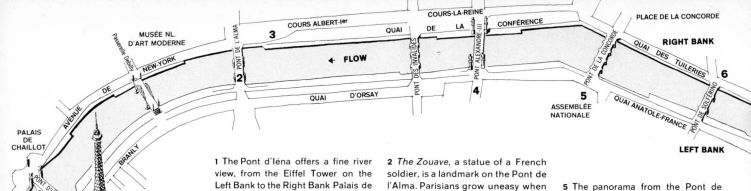

1 The Pont d'Iéna offers a fine river view, from the Eiffel Tower on the Left Bank to the Right Bank Palais de Chaillot. Upstream from this bridge, past the Pont de l'Alma, Robert Fulton tested the first steamboat in 1803.

3 Sight-seeing boats are available on both banks: *Bateaux Mouches* dock on the Right, the cheaper *Bateaux Vedettes* are on the Left. The Quai d'Orsay is lined by government buildings.

4 From Pont Alexandre-III are seen the Grand-Palais exposition hall and the Petit-Palais museum on the Right Bank, Les Invalides on the Left Bank.

2 *The Zouave,* a statue of a French soldier, is a landmark on the Pont de l'Alma. Parisians grow uneasy when the Seine rises to the statue's feet.

5 The panorama from the Pont de la Concorde is spectacular. To the north, beyond the Madeleine and the Place de la Concorde, Sacré-Coeur glows above Montmartre. The Palais-Bourbon, home of the National Assembly, squats above public swimming-pool barges on the Left Bank.

6 On the Right Bank, just before the Louvre, are the Tuileries Gardens. Across is Quai Anatole France with its Palais de la Légion d'Honneur.

A WALK ALONG THE RIVER, BACK INTO HISTORY

Many of Paris' noblest landmarks and finest vistas are crowded into the central half of the Seine's winding course through the city limits. For all of its sights, the area mapped above is not too great for a leisurely afternoon's stroll, but most visitors will want to come to the Seine as Parisians do, for short walks by day or night. (Elsewhere in this guide detailed information is provided on many of the landmarks identified on the map above.) From the Pont d'Iéna to the Pont Royal, 7, the Right Bank (*top*) is more interesting than the Left. If the walker follows the map numbers in order he will be moving backward into history, from recent structures to the stately Renaissance homes around

7 The Pont du Carrousel is at the geographic center of Paris; upon the Pont des Arts footbridge, benches give a fine view of the Île de la Cité.

9 Pont Neuf, the oldest bridge, cuts across Île de la Cité between the Square du Vert-Galant and the Palais de Justice, next to the Conciergerie.

10 An open-air market where flowers and birds are sold is close to the Conciergerie, just across from the quay devoted to gardening supplies.

11 The towers of the Hôtel de Ville on the Right Bank, the imposing north side of Notre-Dame on the Île de la Cité, and the peaceful Île St-Louis are all visible from the Pont d'Arcole.

12 From Île St-Louis, the cruciform design of Notre-Dame is most clearly evident. Île St-Louis, a quiet residential area with narrow streets and shady quays, looks much as it did 300 years ago. Until the 17th Century it was two smaller, bridgeless islands on whose meadows duelists fought.

13 Two mansions, called *hôtels* and named after early residents De Lauzun and Lambert, are the most imposing buildings on Île St-Louis. The island owes its harmonious architecture to gifted planning. Started in 1627, building was practically completed in 50 years. Stately facades, wrought-iron balconies and enclosed courts adorn its homes, where resided Gautier, Daumier and Baudelaire.

8 The famous bookstalls appear here on the Left Bank and continue upstream intermittently on both banks. Along the Quais Voltaire and Malaquais, where great writers lived, there are quality book and antique stores.

Map labels:

LOUVRE
PONT ROYAL
QUAI VOLTAIRE
QUAI DU LOUVRE
QUAI MALAQUAIS
PONT DU CARROUSEL
PONT DES ARTS
Geographic Center of Paris
Square du Vert-Galant
ÉCOLE DES BEAUX-ARTS
L'INSTITUT DE FRANCE
QUAI DE CONTI
PONT NEUF
QUAI DES GRANDS-AUGUSTINS
LATIN QUARTER
QUAI ST-MICHEL
PONT ST-MICHEL
PETIT-PONT
QUAI DE LA MÉGISSERIE
QUAI AU CHANGE
PONT NOTRE-DAME
Sainte-Chapelle
ÎLE DE LA CITÉ
PONT D'ARCOLE
HÔTEL DE VILLE
NOTRE-DAME
QUAI DE L'HÔTEL-DE-VILLE
PONT LOUIS-PHILIPPE
PONT ST-LOUIS
QUAI AU DOUBLE
PONT AU DOUBLE
QUAI DE MONTEBELLO
PONT DE L'ARCHEVÊCHÉ
QUAI DE LA TOURNELLE
PONT DE LA TOURNELLE
PONT MARIE
QUAI DES CÉLESTINS
ÎLE ST-LOUIS
Hôtel de Lauzun
Hôtel Lambert
PONT SULLY

the Pont Neuf, **9**, which since 1604 has linked both banks to the island fortress of ancient Paris. Along the way he will see such traditional sights as the green stalls where books and prints have been sold for 400 years. And from the tree-lined quays it is never far to a sidewalk café and restful refreshment that renews the pleasure of the walk.

A TESTAMENT OF FAITH
IN GLASS AND STONE

All distances from Paris to the borders are measured from the square in front of Notre-Dame (*map, pages 26-27, R-3*) and all French roads run toward it. The cathedral grew with the French through a period that saw the birth of Paris as a religious, political and commercial center, and out of a need for a church big enough to serve an expanding population. Abiding witness to the medieval veneration of the Virgin, the church is also, in Victor Hugo's words, an expression "of human creation, mighty and fertile as the Divine." This Gothic structure rose in three stages, from 1163 to 1250, during which several thousand workmen labored on it and "expense was sought rather than spared."

But Notre-Dame has not been consistently loved. In the 16th Century the French Protestants stormed it. In the 18th Century royal architects replaced much medieval stained glass with clear glass, and during the Revolution mobs toppled its statues and ransacked tombs and altars. In the 19th Century, however, much of its glory was restored and Notre-Dame again became the national church of France.

● *Open every day until 6 p.m.*

The West Facade

TWIN TOWERS, reached by 387 steps, provide exhilarating views of the city sprawled below. From their belfries sound the bells which announce wars, triumphs, funerals and marriages, and which Quasimodo rang in Hugo's famous novel, *The Hunchback of Notre-Dame.*

ROSE WINDOW, sign of Mary, dates from the 13th Century. It has a 32-foot stone frame, the lightness and the strength of which have never been duplicated. In front of it stands a statue of the Virgin, adorned during the Middle Ages with gold and painted many bright colors.

THREE PORTALS, named, from left to right, the Virgin's, the Judgment and St. Anne's, are richly decorated. The Judgment shows the dead rising from the grave, while St. Anne's includes a portrait of Maurice de Sully, the bishop who conceived the plan of the cathedral.

GREAT CATHEDRAL, seen on the opposite page in an aerial photograph, stands regally on the Île de la Cité a few feet from the Seine. Its roofs form a cross, and the ornamented facade, centering on the Virgin, is the accomplishment of an anonymous genius who saw to it that its size, though vast for the time, never overwhelmed the viewer.

33

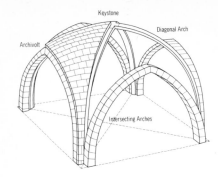

Keystone

Diagonal Arch

Archivolt

Intersecting Arches

RIBBED VAULT, shown at left, is an arched masonry structure developed by Gothic architects. It took the weight of the roof on crisscrossed pointed arches and conveyed the load to supporting columns. This permitted architects to put up higher walls pierced with huge windows.

INSPIRED CONSTRUCTION
OF MASTER BUILDERS

Notre-Dame was built during the years of Gothic architecture's greatest development, when architects were striving to give tangible shape to the medieval ideal of light—"God is light and light gives beauty to things." Builders also wanted high, thin walls. This combination of desires led to the invention of the ribbed vault and flying buttress shown on this page, which made possible the dramatic and spiritual look of the cathedral—both inside and out. The vault and buttress freed walls of their usual roles as supports for the roof by distributing and channeling its weight, and helped stabilize the structure. Thus walls could rise higher than ever before and spaces between columns and pillars could be filled with stained glass to bring in floods of colored light.

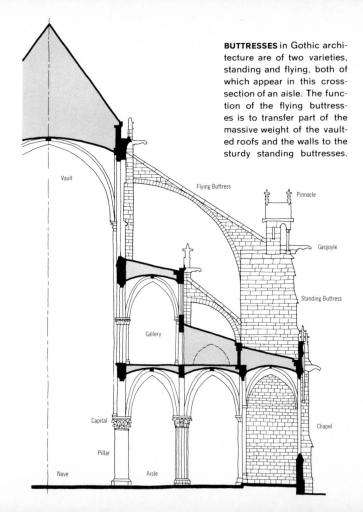

BUTTRESSES in Gothic architecture are of two varieties, standing and flying, both of which appear in this cross-section of an aisle. The function of the flying buttresses is to transfer part of the massive weight of the vaulted roofs and the walls to the sturdy standing buttresses.

Vault

Flying Buttress

Pinnacle

Gargoyle

Standing Buttress

Gallery

Capital

Chapel

Pillar

Nave

Aisle

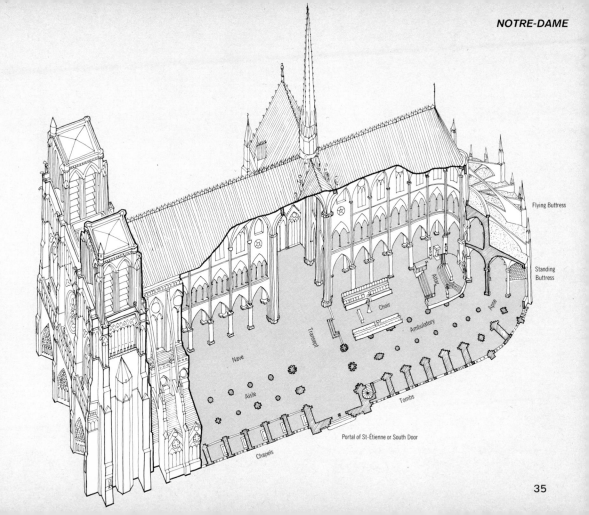

THE INTERIOR of Notre-Dame, with its many vaults supported by buttresses, is shown in this cutaway drawing. Its principal divisions are the nave (flanked by the double aisles); the aisle, called the transept, which cuts across to form the arms of a cross; and the choir, where the high altar stands. Behind the choir is the semicircular area known as the apse. The apse of Notre-Dame, with its elegant vaults and columns, is considered to be especially beautiful.

Flying Buttress

Standing Buttress

Choir

Ambulatory

Apse

Transept

Nave

Aisle

Tombs

Portal of St-Étienne or South Door

Chapels

35

A SANCTUARY FOR "THE GREATEST DEEDS"

Notre-Dame has been described by a Frenchman as "the living witness of all the greatest deeds of our national existence, of our sadnesses and joys." Here nearly every significant event in France has received religious sanction. Great men have come here for *Te Deum* celebrations: kings after their coronations at Rheims; Charles VII upon the recapture of Paris from the English, six years after Henry VI of England had himself been crowned King of France in the cathedral; a grateful Louis XIII on the birth of the son who was to be Louis XIV. More recently heroes like Marshal Foch have been paid last honors here. When Paris was liberated from the Nazis in August 1944, a detachment of tanks drove to the cathedral square, and Free French soldiers scrambled up the tower stairs to ring the oldest of the bells, the famous Emmanuel. On May 9, 1945, a *Te Deum* was sung in Notre-Dame to mark the end of World War II.

A MEMORIAL MASS in Notre-Dame honors Marshal Jacques-Philippe Leclerc, leader of the Second French Armored Division, whose tanks were first to enter Paris August 25, 1944. Leclerc died in a crash in 1947.

CORONATION SCENE in Notre-Dame on December 2, 1804 (*opposite*), shows Napoleon, in the famous David painting, crowning Josephine. He had previously taken his crown from the Pope and crowned himself.

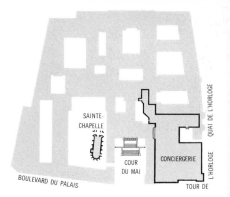

ORNATE CLOCK of the Conciergerie (*left*), at the Quai de l'Horloge, is where Paris' first public clock told time in Charles V's era, about 1370.

HISTORIC MAZE shown on locator map (*right*) holds Palais de Justice, with the Sainte-Chapelle in a court and the Conciergerie at lower right.

A DREAD FORTRESS
AND COURT OF JUSTICE

The heavy cluster of old walls and turrets occupying the western end of the Île de la Cité is lightened only by the crystalline delicacy of the Sainte-Chapelle (*pages 40-43*). Housing the French law courts is the hulking Palais de Justice (*map, pages 26-27, P-1*), which stands on the site of the palace of the early Roman governors of Paris. Little of the Conciergerie's original form has survived two major fires, but its medieval towers still exude memories of the Middle Ages, when they contained torture chambers and dungeons where prisoners were left in pits to be attacked by rats.

• *The Conciergerie is open 10-12 and 1:30 to 5 except Tuesdays.*

CELL BLOCK where Marie Antoinette was imprisoned in the Conciergerie is seen at left. Some of the unfortunate queen's possessions are on exhibit in the chapel. The Conciergerie is still used for prisoners who are awaiting trial in the Palais de Justice.

LAWYERS in their gowns and hats converse in one of the Palais de Justice's long corridors (*right*). One of a series of satirical 19th Century drawings and paintings by Daumier, the scene is still a familiar one, as lawyers wear the very same robes today.

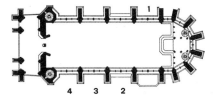

THE SOARING GLORIES
OF THE SAINTE-CHAPELLE

The Sainte-Chapelle (*map, pages 26-27, P-1*) is flooded with color. You walk into its upper chapel and bathe in color. It is other things too—one of the great Gothic treasures of the 13th Century, the private chapel of kings and the shrine where sacred relics were once kept. But its glory is the 1,134 stained glass scenes, all warm and aglow, that illustrate the Old and New Testament stories and the Passion of Christ.

● *Open 10 to 12, 1:30 to 6, from April 1 to September 30; to 5 from October 1 to March 31. Closed Tuesdays and holidays.*

1 JERICHO INVASION windows (*right, top panel*) shows the Jews under Joshua carrying the Ark of the Covenant as they prepare to cross the river Jordan. Below, Joshua's spies are seen departing for Jericho.

MASTER WINDOWS
OF AN AGE OF FAITH

2 MORDECAI, in the story of Esther (*left*), warns Esther of a plot against King Ahasuerus. The upper panels portray the conspirators conniving.

3 DAVID, triumphant after stunning Goliath (*below*) with his slingshot, redeems the promise he made to him to "take thine head from thee."

4 ROSE WINDOW shows a display at the Sainte-Chapelle of a sacred relic (*left*) allegedly the true crown of thorns worn by Christ. Louis IX acquired this from the Emperor of Constantinople plus bits of wood believed to be parts of the true Cross. Subsidiary circles in the window depict several reverent figures watching this display.

ANCIENT STOREHOUSE
FOR A WEALTH OF LEARNING

No American will ever fully understand French universities; you have to be born in France. But it may be helpful to know that the great University of Paris started in the 12th Century, with students sitting on straw in the streets of the Latin Quarter listening to a famous scholar named Abélard, whose works are still studied. In succeeding centuries the University of Paris never acquired a campus or regular courses as we know them. It subdivided into a number of colleges. Best known to Americans in Paris is the Sorbonne (*map, pages 26-27, 0-6*), named for its founder, Robert de Sorbon. Greatest scholastically is the Collège de France, founded by François I. The Collège has no entrance requirements, no degrees, no tuition, no required courses and optional final exams. Nowhere in the world do students have more freedom to acquire "learning that chases away the darkness and reveals . . . the secrets of Knowledge."

A TREASURY of art, old manuscripts and literature is contained in the Bibliothèque Ste-Geneviève. The huge reading room of the library (*opposite*) seats 650; permission to work there is simple to obtain.

FIRST WOMAN allowed to teach a course at the Sorbonne, Madame Pierre Curie, co-discoverer of radium, is shown at right giving her unprecedented demonstration and lecture on radioactivity in November 1906.

A WALK THROUGH
THE MEDIEVAL CITY
OF STUDENTS

Although marked by no visible walls or boundaries, the Latin Quarter (so named because Latin was the language spoken in the university until the French Revolution) is as separate from the rest of Paris as a moated medieval city. It has been the special fiefdom of students at the Sorbonne, heart of the University of Paris, since the 13th Century. Many of them still live in its little hotels around the Rue St-Jacques, which was once a Roman highway. They buy books in its musty old bookstores, eat in its crowded *bistros* that spread cooking odors through its twisting ancient streets. They linger in its cafés. They no longer speak Latin, but they speak all the languages of Europe, along with Arabic, Chinese and obscure dialects of Africa. Above all, they roam what is now the major artery of their private preserve, the Boulevard St-Michel, or "Boul Mich." A walk through the Latin Quarter is a walk through a great teeming intellectual labyrinth, centuries old. This tour takes about one hour if you walk quickly, but with judicious pauses, it could become a full day's well-spent promenade.

● *For admission to public buildings, see page 157.*

1 Place St-Michel is the point of departure for this walk. Visitors can meet at the Boule-d'Or or the Taverne du Palais on the Place and glimpse some of the Latin Quarter students at the edge of their domain.

2 From the boulevard turn into the Rue de la Huchette, an ancient alley with buildings unchanged for centuries. Napoleon supposedly lived at No. 10. Arabs and Indo-Chinese live here, and El Djazair at No. 27 features mint tea and belly dancers. The Théâtre de la Huchette is the smallest theater in Paris. Do look into the famous old Rue du Chat-qui-Pêche, shortest street in Paris.

3 Retrace your steps to the Rue de la Harpe, with its venerable houses, and then continue to Rue St-Séverin for a look at its charming 16th Century Gothic Church of St-Séverin.

4 Take Rue de la Parcheminerie to Rue St-Jacques, then right to Rue St-Julien-le-Pauvre. At No. 16 is the Musée des Trois Mailletz, with its collection of instruments of torture exhibited in ancient cellars.

5 The Church of St-Julien-le-Pauvre, on the street of the same name, dates from the 12th Century. Its park has a lovely view of Notre-Dame, and one of the oldest trees in Paris. At No. 10 is Le Cris de Paris, a pleasing restaurant. Many little streets nearby are worth exploring, but this tour returns to the Rue Galande, the Rue Lagrange and Place Maubert, with its lush vegetable and fish market.

6 Turn right into the Boulevard St-Germain, left on Rue de Cluny, right on Rue Du Sommerard to the Musée de Cluny. The chapel and Unicorn tapestries are high points.

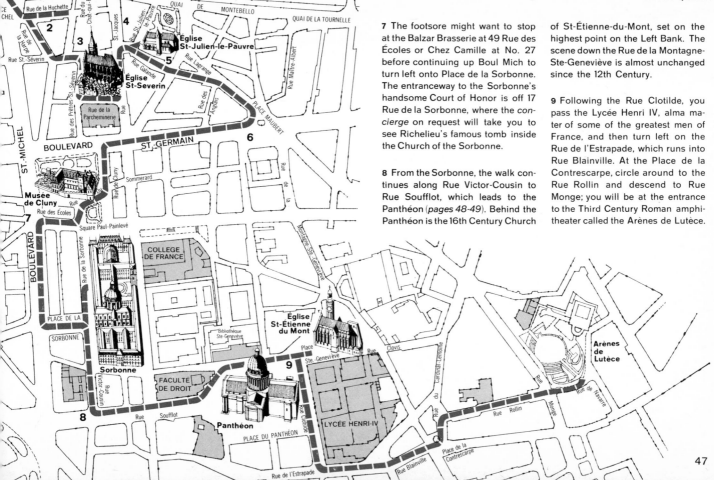

7 The footsore might want to stop at the Balzar Brasserie at 49 Rue des Écoles or Chez Camille at No. 27 before continuing up Boul Mich to turn left onto Place de la Sorbonne. The entranceway to the Sorbonne's handsome Court of Honor is off 17 Rue de la Sorbonne, where the *concierge* on request will take you to see Richelieu's famous tomb inside the Church of the Sorbonne.

8 From the Sorbonne, the walk continues along Rue Victor-Cousin to Rue Soufflot, which leads to the Panthéon (*pages 48-49*). Behind the Panthéon is the 16th Century Church of St-Étienne-du-Mont, set on the highest point on the Left Bank. The scene down the Rue de la Montagne-Ste-Geneviève is almost unchanged since the 12th Century.

9 Following the Rue Clotilde, you pass the Lycée Henri IV, alma mater of some of the greatest men of France, and then turn left on the Rue de l'Estrapade, which runs into Rue Blainville. At the Place de la Contrescarpe, circle around to the Rue Rollin and descend to Rue Monge; you will be at the entrance to the Third Century Roman amphitheater called the Arènes de Lutèce.

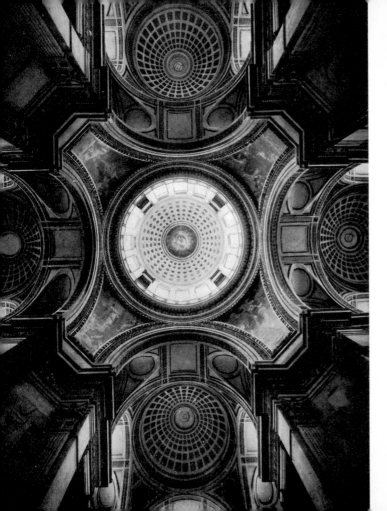

A RESTING PLACE FOR HEROES

In the Panthéon (*map, pages 26-27, P-7*), among 57 other great Frenchmen, lie Victor Hugo and Émile Zola, Louis Braille, who developed the system of printing and writing for the blind that bears his name, and André Maginot of World War II's ill-fated Maginot Line. Begun in 1764 as a church dedicated to Ste Geneviève, patron saint of Paris, in 1791 this classical building was turned into a mausoleum and declared a Temple of Fame by the Revolutionary Parliament. But the first of "the great men of the epoch of French liberty" to be buried in it, the Comte de Mirabeau, was later considered to have been too close to the monarchy and his bones were removed. The 425-step climb to the top of the dome is justified by the 360-degree view of Paris and a close-up of the adjacent 12th Century Tower of Clovis.

● *Open 10-12, 1:30-4 (6 in summer). Guided tours are made to the crypt every 15 minutes. Closed Tuesdays and holidays.*

THE GREAT DOME of the Panthéon, seen from directly underneath, is decorated with frescoes commissioned by Napoleon. The dome was used in 1851 for an experiment to prove that the earth rotates.

A FULL-DRESS CORTEGE conveys the bones of the great philosopher Voltaire to the Panthéon in 1791. The esteem this shrine once enjoyed has decreased, perhaps because of the coldness of its vast interior.

"CAFÉ FILTRE," coffee made at the table with an individual filter (*left*), is one of several versions of this pungent staple you can order in Parisian cafés.

A PRETTY GIRL neglects her friends to exercise one of the prerogatives of café life, doing whatever pleases one best, which in her case is dreaming.

THE FRENCHMAN'S
EXTRA LIVING ROOM

A Frenchman once asked an American, "How do Americans live without cafés? Where do they meet their friends? Where do they take their girl friends after the cinema? Where do they take their wives and children?" His perplexity was understandable: there is one café for every 173 Frenchmen. Of these thousands of cafés, ranging from homey neighborhood spots to boulevard show places, the liveliest are those of St-Germain des Prés. The most famous of these are shadowed by the church that gave the district its name. Under the awnings of intellectual hangouts like Deux Magots and Flore are crowded tables once used by the painter Pablo Picasso and the philosopher Jean-Paul Sartre and many another famous name. Here sit the young and not-so-young, arguing, sipping, dreaming, chatting, holding hands.

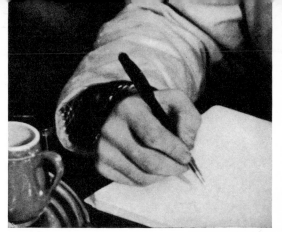

A PLAY OF HANDS in various cafés of St-Germain des Prés tells much about the people who go there. A student does his homework at a table (*above*) because his cramped room is too cold and dismal. Lovers (*above, right*) restrain their impatience; the man, wearing the glove, is ready to leave. A ballet of expressive fingers (*right*) reveals the whimsey of another couple.

A WALK
THROUGH VIBRANT
ST-GERMAIN DES PRÉS

The streets, alleys and courts mapped on the opposite page bustle with students, painters, businessmen, literary types, housewives, models; with aggressive, bumper-to-bumper traffic; with antique shops, bookstores, print shops and art galleries. Here is a chance to see the artistic and intellectual life of Paris close up. Much history has been made in the crowded streets, and the addresses of famous men of the past abound. Artists and students like to live here. Some have been attracted by the august École des Beaux-Arts; others by the round-the-clock spectacle of café life.

The walk should take a good hour without stops, as long as you like if you want to linger. Anyone taking it at night will find that many of the antique shops, bookstores and art galleries stay open from 7:30 until 11:00 p.m. and welcome browsers. Knowledgeable shoppers can find bargains here, especially if they are willing to gamble on the futures of young artists. Night is a good time to drop in at cafés like Deux Magots and Flore, or the popular La Rhumerie Martiniquaise, all on the animated Boulevard St-Germain.

● *For admission to public buildings mentioned, see page 157.*

1 Begin at Rue Bonaparte. To the left on the Quai Malaquais is the Institut de France, home of five famous academies, one of which is the Académie Française, guardian of the French language. Walking down Rue Bonaparte, where antique shops cluster, note the École des Beaux-Arts. In the Rue des Beaux-Arts there are no fewer than 12 art galleries. Follow the marked route into Rue de l'Abbaye.

2 Turn right off Rue de l'Abbaye and amble down the crooked Rue Cardinale to Place de Furstenberg, one of the most charming squares in Paris, whose very romantic setting amidst ornate lampposts and magnolia trees recalls another day. The 19th Century painter Delacroix lived at No. 6 and worked in the studio behind the house. Take a look at the antique shop called Yveline.

3 Return to Rue de l'Abbaye and continue to Place St-Germain-des-Prés, site of Paris' oldest church, which is well worth a visit. Nearby are found some of the best-known of the intellectual cafés, and also two fine restaurants—Calvet at 165 Boulevard St-Germain for lunch or dinner and the Brasserie Lipp at 151, good at any time but especially interesting after theater at night when notables drop in.

4 Cross the Boulevard St-Germain and go up Rue des Ciseaux, a street of dilapidated houses. To the right, on the corner of Rue Gozlin, there is a delightful French toy store, Le Berceau de France, where you may want to shop. Follow the marked route to the Church of St-Sulpice, second largest in Paris. It boasts one of the finest organs in France. The entrance is on Rue Palatine.

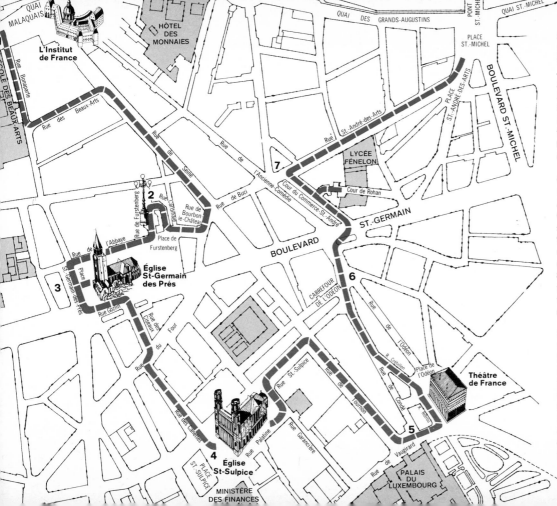

5 At the corner where Rue St-Sul-pice meets the Rue de Tournon, turn right. Balzac lived at No. 2, and John Paul Jones, naval hero of the American Revolution, died at No. 19. A left turn into Rue Vaugirard brings into view the Palais du Luxembourg. Rue Rotrou on the left leads into the Place de l'Odéon. The theater here houses a company that gives modern and classic dramas.

6 The Carrefour de l'Odéon is a magnet for students, and a busy *Métro* stop. Cross the Boulevard St-Germain again and enter the Passage du Commerce-St-André. At No. 9, Guillotin tried out his beheading machine; the revolutionary journalist Marat printed his paper at No. 8. In the middle of the Passage is the Cour de Rohan, three small, picturesque courts which retain the atmosphere of yesteryear.

7 At the Carrefour de Buci, turn into the Rue St-André-des-Arts. At No. 43 is Paris' oldest girls' school. In the Rue des Grands-Augustins, to the left, is La Grenouille, a colorful restaurant, at No. 26, and El Catalan, a bar once frequented by Picasso and now a gypsy hangout, at No. 16. This walk comes to an end at Place St-André, a stone's throw from Place St-Michel.

53

A RELAXED PARK
FOR ALL AGES OF MAN

Parisians love parks, and each park in Paris has a dedicated following of its own. The Luxembourg Gardens (*map, pages 26-27, L-7*) derive a special charm from the Parisians who gather there. One French writer has said that field marshals, inventors and statesmen would be out of place there, but poets and children are in their element. The Luxembourg Gardens have kept only a few features from their earliest

INFANTS OUT FOR AN AIRING in the gardens are wheeled along the quiet dirt paths by mothers and nurses. Set between Montparnasse and the Latin Quarter, the park is a favorite with families of widely varied backgrounds.

MEN AND WOMEN play a popular card game called *belote* on an outdoor table that turns a corner of the Luxembourg Gardens into a club. In this park, all of the ages of man can be seen strolling, reading and playing.

days. The flower beds, the fountain and the central walk are all that remain of the formal, classic French garden that the park was in the days of Marie de Médicis, who founded it in 1615. The rest is a wondrous assortment of unexpected corners, statues and a delightful intimacy surprising in a park that covers 60 acres. Near the center of the gardens is a celebrated puppet theater, the Théâtre du Luxembourg.

BOYS on recess from schools near the gardens (*above*) make the most of snowfall, which is rare in Paris.

STUDENTS loaf and sun (*right*) in front of the Luxembourg Palace, which is now the home of the French Senate.

THE HAUNT OF WRITERS
AND PAINTERS

Intellectual ferment and the tumult of the artistic-bohemian life are found in many parts of Paris, but nowhere more than in Montparnasse. The heart of the neighborhood is where the boulevards Raspail and Montparnasse cross (*map, pages 26-27, J-9*). This is the site of famous cafés: the Dôme, Select, Coupole and Rotonde (the last is now a movie house). At the sidewalk tables of these cafés before World War I the painter Amedeo Modigliani and the writer André Gide took their afternoon *apéritifs*. About that time Lenin and Trotsky were here, too, plotting over tea. Between the two world wars, these cafés were headquarters for such writers as Ernest Hemingway, Scott Fitzgerald and Sherwood Anderson, and such painters as Picasso, Matisse and Braque. Montparnasse is perhaps less tumultuous now, but the aspiring painters at least are still here: by day, working; by night, in the cafés in impassioned discussions.

PROTESTING AMERICAN ARTISTS at the Select café voice indignation at the rejection of their paintings by a committee setting up an exhibit. Their hot protests persuaded a new committee to reverse the verdict.

A STUDENT SCULPTRESS fashions a clay figure from life at the Grande Chaumière, foremost of Montparnasse's art schools. Models at this school and others are often university students.

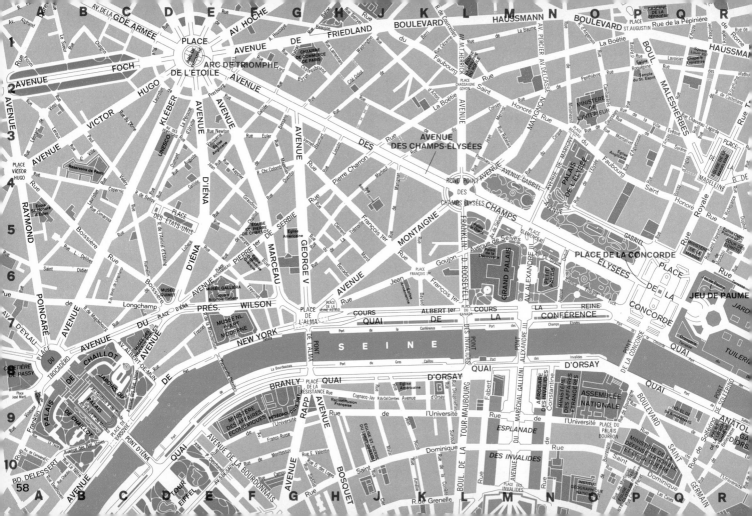

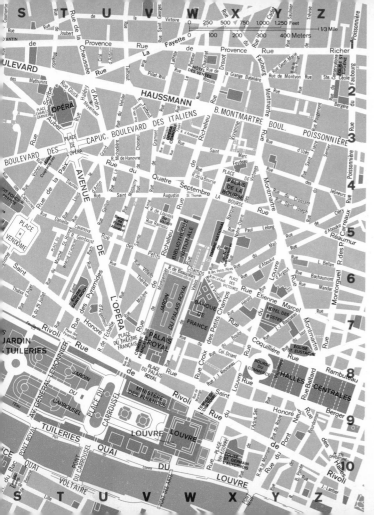

2

IMAGES
OF
GLORY

Along the Right Bank, between the Étoile and the Place de la Concorde, Paris is a city where great human aspirations and accomplishments are magnificently memorialized. Martial glory is represented by the massive yet soaring Arc de Triomphe, which Napoleon ordered built in 1806 to honor France's conquering armies. Artistic glory illuminates the Louvre, whose cavernous halls house what is generally considered the finest collection of art in the world. And extending half the distance between the two is the Champs-Élysées, equally famed as the meeting place of Paris and as "the triumphal way." This elegant avenue unfolds an architectural panorama which itself is a monument to man, the builder of cities.

HIGHLIGHTS shown in red (*left*) are covered in detail in the following pages; other points of interest in this area appear in black.

A PRINCELY PALACE
FOR TREASURES OF ART

So vast and varied are the treasures of the Louvre that an unprepared visitor can emerge from it more bewildered than enriched. But with careful selection (such as was made for the tours described on the following pages) this collection of collections can be enjoyed. The Louvre was once a royal palace. The stately Grande Galerie section, where the *Mona Lisa* hangs, first housed the royal mint, a tapestry factory and a group of workers in precious metals. When Louis XIII was Dauphin, he exercised his pet camel in it; as king he paraded through it in healing rituals for the sick. After Louis XIV moved the court out to Versailles, the Louvre became a camping ground for squatters' tents, prostitutes and pickpockets. It was Napoleon, whose foreign conquests included many works of art, who established the Louvre as a museum.

● *Open 10 to 5 every day except Tuesdays and holidays. Evening schedules vary; see newspaper listings.*

A STATELY COMPLEX of majestic buildings, the Louvre is built around acres of formal gardens. At left center is the pink marble Arch of the Carrousel, built between 1806 and 1808 to honor Napoleonic triumphs.

FORTY-FIVE CENTURIES
OF GLORIOUS ART

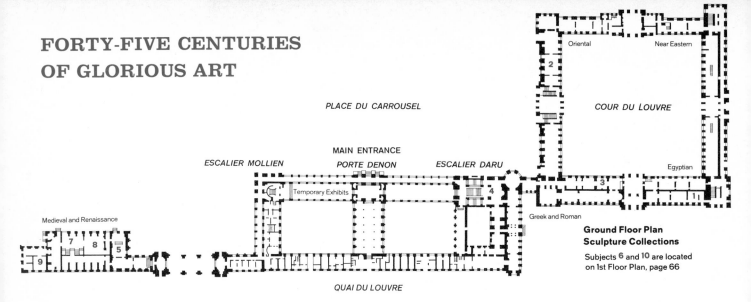

PLACE DU CARROUSEL

COUR DU LOUVRE

Oriental   Near Eastern

MAIN ENTRANCE

ESCALIER MOLLIEN   PORTE DENON   ESCALIER DARU

Egyptian

Temporary Exhibits

Medieval and Renaissance

Greek and Roman

**Ground Floor Plan
Sculpture Collections**

Subjects **6** and **10** are located
on 1st Floor Plan, page 66

QUAI DU LOUVRE

Of the thousands of beautiful objects in the Louvre, 30 masterpieces of sculpture and painting are shown on the following pages. The location of each of them is keyed into the floor plans above and on page 66 to make it easier to find any specific work. These works of art are considered by experts at the Louvre and at New York's Metropolitan Museum worthy of being ranked among the finest treasures in the Louvre. The visitor with limited time to spend should see at least these works.

A number appears beside the description of each work,

and again as a locator on the floor plan above. By following the numbers in order, a visitor will be guided through the Louvre on a chronological, step-saving tour that touches 10 high points in the long and majestic history of sculpture.

In sculpture, the Louvre's collections of ancient art are more distinguished than its works from the Renaissance. It is the richest of all museums in middle eastern antiquities. Its celebrated Greek department includes both the *Venus de Milo* and the *Winged Victory of Samothrace,* which are probably the two best-known statues in the world.

Sculpture of the Ancient World

1 **"SEATED SCRIBE,"** a superb figure from Egypt's Old Kingdom around 2500 B.C., is a lifelike portrayal of an ordinary man in sharp contrast to the idealized images of gods and kings that are typical of Egyptian art. The scribe's quartz eyes and ebony pupils are inlaid in limestone with great artistry. They convey an expression of intelligence and keen expectation.

2 **"GUDEA SEATED,"** a serene statuette in hard green stone, portrays the benignant priest-king who ruled the city of Lagash in Sumer around 2450 B.C. To remind the gods of his faithful service, Gudea had many such images placed in temples. The Louvre has parts of 10 that survived the fall of Sumer, as well as a group of clay cylinders describing Gudea's great works.

3 **"VENUS DE MILO,"** whose popularity is as great as its noble beauty, is the subject of continuing debate among critics. Most agree the statue is finer because its arms are missing. Efforts to date its body, which was excavated in two pieces in 1820, have produced estimates from as early as the Fifth Century B.C. to as late as 90 B.C. in more recent opinions.

4 **"WINGED VICTORY,"** discovered on Samothrace in 1862, looms boldly on its stone prow atop the Louvre's grand staircase. It was carved early in the Hellenistic epoch, which started with Alexander's death in 323 B.C. and ended with the fall of Greece in 146 B.C. Typical of that period, it combines calm Greek classicism with richer, more turbulent eastern style.

63

Medieval piety and Renaissance vigor

5 **FUNERARY MONUMENT,** a stylized expression of the Middle Ages' pervasive concern with death, is a great masterpiece of Gothic art. Philippe Pot, Grand Seneschal of Burgundy, was the man whose stone effigy and coats of arms are borne by the figures of cloaked retainers. Their bereavement is represented with power and intense realism–a departure from the restrained emotion of classical Greek art.

6 **RELIQUARY** known as the Crown of St. Louis (*plan, page 66*) is a beautiful curiosity designed to contain holy relics. Glittering with angels and fleurs-de-lis, it exemplifies the power and the piety alike of its donor, King Louis IX. The king, who dedicated his life to keeping peace among Christians and warring on the infidels, died on a crusade and was canonized in 1297.

7 **STRUGGLING SLAVE** by Michelangelo, a portion of which appears above, is one of two seven-foot marbles which portray first the agony and then the wearied acquiescence of a captive. The figures are almost savage in their contortions. In this violent break with classicism, Michelangelo was inspired by Hellenistic art and in turn he inspired baroque art.

French classicism and the baroque

8 **"DIANA OF ANET,"** by 16th Century sculptor Jean Goujon, personifies the elegance and grace of French classicism. This exquisite work was inspired not by the Roman goddess but by a lovely worldling, Diane de Poitiers, mistress of Henri II. Diane, who lived at Anet, identified herself with the goddess of the hunt and inspired numerous other idealized works of art.

9 **BAROQUE BAS-RELIEF,** carved by Pierre Puget with realism unfashionable in his time, interprets a significant encounter between the philosopher Diogenes and Alexander the Great. The detail above shows old Diogenes, interrupted while sunbathing, daring to tell Alexander, on horseback, to move out of the sun. The moral: even the mighty owe respect to philosophers. Still striving for Michelangelo's power rather than classicism's beauty, Puget died in 1694, embittered and out of favor in court circles.

10 **"MADAME HOUDON"** is a bust (*plan, page 66*) of the wife of sculptor Jean-Antoine Houdon, who caught her warmth and charm with informality and obvious affection. Other high points of Houdon's prolific 70-year career include his busts of Voltaire and Diderot, also in the Louvre, and his statue of George Washington, which he sculptured in America in 1788.

THE RICHEST COLLECTION
OF PAINTINGS IN THE WORLD

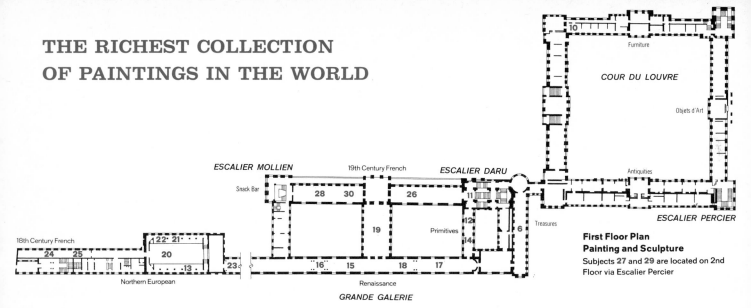

First Floor Plan
Painting and Sculpture
Subjects **27** and **29** are located on 2nd
Floor via Escalier Percier

The Louvre's assemblage of paintings was begun in the 16th Century, when King François I put together a nucleus of 12 Italian masterpieces, including the *Mona Lisa*. Since then its acquisitions have made it the largest and richest museum of paintings in the world. While other museums are more abundantly endowed with the works of an individual artist or even a national school, the value and variety of the Louvre's western paintings are undisputed, and its collection of such immortals as Leonardo da Vinci, Titian, Rembrandt, Rubens and the French masters is unsurpassed. The number of paintings now exhibited in the Louvre and in the nearby Jeu de Paume is 2,200. From this vast store, 25 have been selected for reproduction in this guide. They trace the long history of western painting from a 13th Century masterpiece (*opposite*) by Cimabue, who has been called "one of the first artists to have emerged from the collective anonymity of the Middle Ages," up to a still life by Paul Cézanne, the father of modern art. Of these 25 paintings, those that hang in the principal Louvre building are located by key number in the floor plan above.

66

An age of revival, Gothic to Renaissance

11 **"MADONNA WITH ANGELS,"** a 14-foot-high altarpiece by the 13th Century Florentine Cimabue, is a magnificent milestone in the transition from Byzantine to Gothic art. Its details, from the platelike halos to the expressionless faces of the angels, are all conventions of Byzantine style, formalized and impersonal. But its flowing lines mark the emergence of the Gothic style and thus the beginning of modern European painting.

12 **"CORONATION OF THE VIRGIN,"** an altarpiece by Fra Angelico painted around 1435, heralds the Renaissance with its freshness of color and complicated composition. Fra Angelico, who was so pious he could not paint a crucifix without tears in his eyes, was beatified after death.

13 **"PIETÀ,"** a 15th Century panel by an unknown French master of the School of Avignon, combines Flemish realism with Byzantine simplicity in what has been called "one of the supreme manifestations of Christian art." This is a reproduction of the major segment of the painting, which has been warped by age.

14 "THE CRUCIFIXION," an early Renaissance masterpiece by Andrea Mantegna, generates its power with converging lines, painstaking detail and a deep background that is romantically imaginative yet convincingly real. As one overawed critic has said of it, "the horror of the scene in this inhuman world becomes so harsh and tragic as to be almost insupportable."

15 "MADONNA" by Raphael glows with the purity and transparent freshness that made his ideal women a measure of feminine beauty. Painted in 1507, it shows the Christ child with His arm gracefully linked to the Virgin's, while the infant St. John looks on in adoration. According to one contemporary account, Raphael possessed the same sweetness of character he put into his paintings: "even the very animals followed his steps and . . . loved him."

16 "MONA LISA," also called *La Gioconda* after the noblewoman believed to have posed for it, is the most familiar work of Leonardo da Vinci's genius— and the most famous painting of all time. Its meaning and the lady's wisp of a smile have provoked endless speculation. Today *Mona Lisa* is probably the most valued and valuable of all the world's art treasures.

the Italian Renaissance

17 **"RUSTIC CONCERT,"** probably by Giorgione, displays in this detail the sensuousness and the refinement of Renaissance art at its height. Little is known of Giorgione's life, but his style pervaded art in 16th Century Venice. Out of 70 paintings sometimes attributed to him, only a handful are incontestably his.

18 **"MAN WITH GLOVE"** by Titian, the most versatile Venetian artist, is one of many portraits of "true children of the Renaissance, whom life has taught no meannesses and fears." In his 99 years of life, Titian produced a prodigious number of imperishable works in great variety.

19 **"MARRIAGE AT CANA"** by Paolo Veronese, a detail from which appears above, presents the Biblical feast as a worldly extravagance. This is the Louvre's largest painting, more than 20 feet high by 30 feet wide, and is crowded with 132 figures, including the artist (playing a viola) and his friends. For mixing the secular and the holy in another painting, Veronese had to answer charges of sacrilege before an Inquisition court.

The flesh and the spirit in Flemish and Dutch painting

20 **"MARIE DE MÉDICIS,"** seen landing at Marseilles, displays Peter Paul Rubens at his most opulent. In this detail from the sixth of 21 huge canvases celebrating Marie's life, she disembarks from her galley as Henri IV's bride on November 3, 1600, and gods and nymphs dance a wild welcome. A master at 20, Rubens spent 43 years lavishing his genius on robust elaborations of the baroque. He is known as the happiest and worldliest of successes in art.

21 **"PILGRIMS AT EMMAUS,"** Rembrandt's portrayal of two disciples recognizing Christ resurrected, conveys a somber mystical hush. Near the end of his life (1606-1669), having realized the depths of poverty and the zenith of achievement, Rembrandt created a series of glorious studies of Jesus Christ.

22 **"THE LACE-MAKER,"** believed to have been Jan Vermeer's wife, shows the painstaking patience that characterizes Vermeer's art. This picture's small size, 10 inches high by 9 inches wide, deepens its sense of intimacy and of the poetry of humble labor. The pale pearly glow on the woman's hands and forehead is typical of Vermeer's effects with light which excited and inspired the Impressionists. Of the sparse production of Vermeer's 43 years (1632-1675), some 30 paintings survive.

A period when subtle Frenchmen put a high finish on art

23 **"INSPIRATION OF THE POET"** by Nicholas Poussin (1594-1665) depicts Apollo, with a muse and cupids, about to bestow laurels on a poet writing under his patronage. Poussin, "the first . . . and most French" of great French painters, typifies classicism in his emphasis on formal harmonies, his restraint in mood and color, and his fondness for mythological themes.

24 **"GILLES,"** a classical buffoon in the Italian *commedia dell' arte,* has a wistful air in Watteau's picture. The painting, reputedly rescued from use as a signboard, sums up the subtle and graceful charm of Watteau. In his brief life (1684-1721) he refined baroque style into rococo; he is immortal as a poet in paint.

25 **STILL LIFE** entitled *Pipe and Drinking Glasses* is one of the many painted by Jean-Baptiste-Siméon Chardin, whose work enhanced this humble Dutch genre and won him the name of "the little Dutchman of the Parisian school." Because Chardin was less interested in representing his subjects than in organizing forms into harmonious composition, he has also been called "the first of the moderns." Though successful in his time, Chardin's greatest recognition came in the esteem of later artists and in his influence on their work.

71

26 **"THE OATH OF THE HORATII"** illustrates Louis David's turn from the rococo style to classical subjects. It shows a Roman father swearing his sons to fight to the death against the city which the husbands of his daughters (*right*) are pledged to defend. Like his paintings, David's life (1748-1825) reflected the changing times: he was a leading figure during the Revolution, "first painter" to Napoleon and an exile after the Bourbons' return.

27 **"LA GRANDE ODALISQUE"** is one of several lush studies in which Jean-Auguste-Dominique Ingres (1780-1867) painted models posing as harem slaves. Here the form is elongated to accentuate its sinuous grace. A student of David's but more influenced by Raphael's classicism, Ingres became a virtual dictator of art after 1825 and a bitter opponent of romantic painting, whose exponents he called "apostles of the ugly."

28 **"JULY 28, 1830"** by Eugène Delacroix celebrates the spirit of revolt in this curious mixture of realism and allegory painted in 1831, a year after the Revolution that inspired it. The painting depicts Liberty leading the people over the slain, with the towers of Notre-Dame in the background. A master of clashing colors and the surging line, a virtuoso with "a sun in his head and storms in his heart," Delacroix became undisputed leader of the romantic movement. Out of his travels and literary interests came many exotic and turbulent paintings.

29 **"WOMAN IN BLUE,"** painted by Jean-Baptiste-Camille Corot a year before his death in 1875, "combines," said one critic, "a solid construction and a delicacy of tone reminiscent of Vermeer" (*page 70*). Though Corot did 323 figure studies, most in the mature style of his later years, he thought of himself as a painter of landscapes. His dying words were: "See how beautiful it is! I have never seen such wonderful scenery."

30 **"THE PAINTER'S STUDIO"** by Gustave Courbet portrays the artist at work in this small detail of a large canvas. Courbet, once described as "probably the most hated, misunderstood and exasperating artist of the 19th Century," strongly influenced Manet through his realistic approach (*next pages*).

SELF-PORTRAIT by Vincent van Gogh suggests the torment that drove the artist to suicide. His painting far outdistanced Impressionism in its boldness of technique and swirling line.

"ORANGES AND APPLES" by Cézanne displays an angularity that was developed by Cubism. Unlike the Impressionists, Cézanne was more interested in form than in color for its own sake.

A BURST OF COLOR
HERALDING A NEW VISION

The climax of a Louvre visit is the Jeu de Paume, whose paintings extend the Louvre's collection into the 20th Century. Here, and in exhibits which are staged at the nearby Orangerie, are the rainbow visions of modern masters.
● *Open 10 to 12:45, 2 to 5. Closed Tuesdays and holidays.*

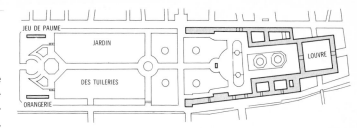

JEU DE PAUME AND ORANGERIE LIE ACROSS THE GARDEN FROM THE LOUVRE

PICNICKERS in Manet's *Luncheon on the Grass* include a nude that shocked the public at the work's first showing.

"REGATTA," painted at Argenteuil, reveals (in this section) Monet's use of color to suggest rather than to depict.

"GIRLS AT PIANO" illustrates Renoir's simple credo of art: that "a painting must be lovable, cheerful and pretty."

75

THE TUILERIES offers a long vista that starts at a decorative pool with little sailing boats and birds (*left*). The eye is carried past the Place de la Concorde and its obelisk along the Champs-Élysées to the looming Arc.

GROWING UP in Paris involves among other things mastery of the merry-go-round. When a boy has achieved the confidence of the intent youngster (*right*) reaching out for the brass ring he is (very nearly) a man.

A CHILD'S EDEN
IN A HISTORIC PARK

No park in Paris is more formal than the Tuileries Gardens (*map, pages 58-59, R-7*), so geometrically precise in their paths, so symmetrical in their flower beds, so right in the middle of town. From August 1792, when Louis XVI and Marie Antoinette fled over the lawns, until the final sacking of the Tuileries Palace during the riots of 1871, the place has known much violent history. One day in 1783, a crowd of 400,000 jammed the gardens to see a man go up in a gas balloon. Today, many grownups come just to rent a chair

CLASSIC PUPPETS are Guignol, the star of every French puppet show, and his plotting pal Gnafron. At right the children listen absorbed as the plot unfolds. Then they break into laughter as the plot collapses and the two characters reach their inevitable comeuppance, ending by batting each other.

(0.25 NF) and bask in the sun. And for children it is ideal. On the prancing chargers of portable merry-go-rounds a boy finds his courage; watching Guignol and Gnafron plot and battle in a thousand puppet shows he learns laughter; sailing a boat to all corners of the world in the pools he stirs his imagination. And here some children begin to learn the little snobberies (for French nursemaids are very careful about the bloodlines and financial status of the children their charges may play with) that will later rule their lives.

COLONNADES, BALUSTRADES AND PERILOUS TRAFFIC

So tremendous is the Place de la Concorde (*map, pages 58-59, Q-6*) that it seems to open and ventilate the entire city. With fountains, bleached balustrades and colonnades, the grand serenity of its proportions makes it one of the greatest squares in the world. Louis XV ordered the square designed to accommodate a statue of himself. Rioting crowds tore down the statue in the Revolution, when the Place was the site of the guillotine that beheaded Louis XVI and Marie Antoinette. In 1836 Louis-Philippe embellished the square with an Egyptian obelisk of the 13th Century B.C.

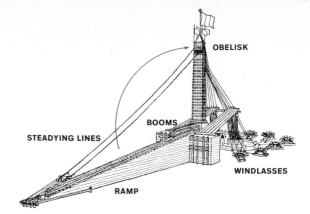

RAISING OF THE OBELISK is recorded on a drawing carved into its base. The crated monolith, 75 feet tall, was inched up the ramp horizontally, then brought upright in an arc (*blue line*) by men turning windlasses.

PLACE LOUIS XV, as it was called at first, is shown in an old print (*above*). The statue is gone, but the two buildings to the north are still there. The Hotel Crillon is at the left and the Ministère de la Marine (the navy) at right.

A GLORIOUS SPECTACLE at all hours, the Place de la Concorde (*opposite*) is filled by rush-hour traffic as perilous as any in the world. The square handles 12 lanes of traffic each way, monitored by police but with no traffic lights.

THE TRIUMPHAL WAY

ONE OF THE WORLD'S GREATEST THOROUGHFARES, THE CHAMPS-ÉLYSÉES MAKES A BREATHTAKING

SWEEP TO THE ARC DE TRIOMPHE, THE MILITARY MONUMENT VICTOR HUGO REVERENTLY CALLED A "MASS OF GLORY"

GAUDY GLAMOR
ON THE CHAMPS-ÉLYSÉES

The section of this celebrated tree-lined avenue between the Rond-Point and the Arc de Triomphe led through open country until the 19th Century. Today, movie palaces, garish auto showrooms, night clubs, travel agencies, clothing stores and chrome-trimmed cafés have replaced most of the elegant mansions of the 1850s, where glamorous demimondaines presided over witty salons. Even though the splendor is gone, the enduring spaciousness of the boulevard continues to make it an exciting place to stroll and a fine vantage point from which to observe the flow of Parisian activity.

SHOWGIRLS of the Lido (*right*) in minimal dress adorn elaborate nightclub shows that sometimes include waterfalls and fireworks on the stage.

NEWSPAPERS are posted daily behind glass outside the *Figaro* office at the Rond-Point for the benefit of interested Champs-Élysées passersby.

SUNNY WALKS make the numerous Champs-Élysées outdoor café terraces favored meeting places for leisurely Parisians and tourists alike.

FOUNTAINS at the Rond-Point are illuminated at night and help to re-create some of the romantic glow of pre-neon days on the Champs-Élysées.

WORLD CAPITAL
OF HAUTE COUTURE

She is no more beautiful than other women, and her measurements are no more spectacular, but the Parisian woman has an indefinable quality, acquired at birth and possessed by her grandmother before her, that sets her apart. The word "chic" could have been invented to describe her. Her obsession with taste and style fuels the $15 million-a-year French *couture* industry, much of it in the Champs-Élysées neighborhood. A visitor can sample part of the intriguing world of the great Paris fashion houses by telephoning in advance for seats. (For details, see pages 180-185.) The more successful the collection, the scarcer the space in these perfumed salons, and while you are more welcome if you are a celebrity or intend to buy, nonbuyers can take comfort in knowing that even movie stars and millionaires have been grateful for a spot on the hall stairway.

Most Parisiennes cannot afford the $500-and-up price of a dress from the *haute couture*. But with the help of hard-working local dressmakers, the women of Paris achieve an alluring, highly individual quality which never fails to turn men's heads—which is what they intended doing all along.

PARISIAN MODELS, like their American counterparts, can be spotted by their oversize handbags. These two are sauntering along the Champs-Élysées, which is close to 70 per cent of the top *couturier* houses.

PARIS MODE of the 1760s, modeled on the life-sized doll at left, recalls the long reign of Parisian taste-setting. Marie Antoinette's dressmaker exported her styles on dolls like these and collected orders en route from all the royal courts of Europe.

ELEGANCE and luxury were the hallmark of 19th Century dresses like those *(below)* worn by Parisian ladies of fashion between 1870 and 1880 for a carriage drive through the Bois de Boulogne or a promenade down the broad, elegant Champs-Élysées.

FASHION SHOWINGS at major houses like Dior *(above)* generate as much excitement in Paris as a theater première. Intrigue surrounds the distribution of seats, and their location is an index of prestige.

A STONE HYMN TO GLORY, AND THOSE WHO DIED FOR IT

After Paris was freed in World War II, General Charles de Gaulle of the Free French visited the Arc de Triomphe during his first 24 hours in the city. The most revered patriotic monument, the Arch sits like a massive gem in the Place de l'Étoile (*map, pages 58-59, E-1*). It was begun in 1806.

- *Platform atop the Arch open every day 10 a.m. to 4 p.m. (6 p.m. in summer) except Tuesday.*

THE ÉTOILE, focal point of 12 avenues, is called "the star" because of its shape. The avenues, at left:

1   Av. des Champs-Élysées
2   Av. Marceau
3   Av. d'Iéna
4   Av. Kléber
5   Av. Victor-Hugo
6   Av. Foch
7   Av. de la Grande-Armée
8   Av. Carnot
9   Av. Mac-Mahon
10   Av. de Wagram
11   Av. Hoche
12   Av. de Friedland

The Great East Facade

SHIELDS carved with names of important battles line the Arc's top, 164 feet up. An elevator carries visitors to the top.

A FRIEZE lines the entire width, 148 feet, of the Arc. Made up of hundreds of six-foot-high figures, it shows French armies marching off to battle.

PANELS bordering the curve of the Arc depict two events in French military history: the great battle of Aboukir (*far left*) that France's navy lost to the English in 1798 and the funeral of General Marceau.

STATUES embellish the piers of the Arc. On the right pier is a group by François Rude, portraying the goddess of war calling Frenchmen to arms to defend the nation. The left pier shows the *Triumph of 1810*, by Jean-Pierre Cortot.

AT THE FLAME OF REMEMBRANCE, burning above the tomb of France's Unknown Soldier, a veteran pauses to pay respect. This shrine, directly beneath the Arc de Triomphe, was created by France in 1921 to honor its war dead.

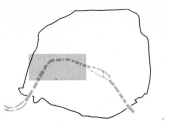

SENTINEL
OF THE
NATION

Along the Left Bank, from the Pont Royal to the spire of the Eiffel Tower, Paris presents to the world its aloof international face—"the French version of a condensed Washington." Here, where conferences of state are held, museums and venerable monuments weave the threads of France's history into the fabric of the present. The National Assembly meets in the Palais Bourbon, begun as a royal retreat and completed in time to be seized by the Revolution. Surrounded by reminders of his imperial glories, Napoleon lies in Les Invalides. And across the river in this area, on the site of a 16th Century Medici mansion, is the Palais de Chaillot, which houses museums linking France to all mankind and Paris to the sea.

HIGHLIGHTS shown in red (*left*) are covered in detail in the following pages; other points of interest in this area appear in black.

CLAMOROUS VOICE
OF THE FRENCH PEOPLE

THE NATIONAL ASSEMBLY BUILDING, the Palais-Bourbon, glows under spotlights. It was Napoleon who had the Greek facade erected, but he is said to have criticized it as being "ridiculous" after getting his first glimpse of it.

In the formal semicircular chamber of the Palais-Bourbon (*map, pages 88-89, S-3*), called the Salle des Séances, meet the 552 deputies of the National Assembly. They come to the capital from all over France and the overseas territories for two sessions a year lasting from October to the middle of December and from the end of April until about July. Together with the Senate, the Assembly is charged with two major functions—those of legislating, and of control and supervision of the government. It has been divided into numerous parties. The impassioned arguments that have raged in the Palais-Bourbon are a reflection of the French electorate's insistence on its individual rights.

The National Assembly traces its descent from the States-General, a prerevolutionary body which included the Three Estates: the clergy, the nobility and the commoners. The commoners, or Third Estate, demanded that all three vote as a single assembly with one ballot per member, and on June 17, 1789, they defiantly proclaimed themselves the National Assembly. A bronze plaque in the Palais-Bourbon shows Mirabeau when he stepped before the States-General and

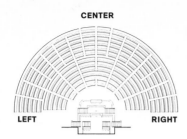

CENTER

LEFT   RIGHT

SEATING plan (*left*) used in the Assembly groups the parties by locations that have taken on political meaning of Right, Left and Center.

IN SESSION, legislators hear Premier Michel Debré. Under the Fifth Republic, the role of the premier has been considerably curtailed.

cried, "We are here by the will of the people, and we shall not leave our places except at the point of the bayonet."

Prior to the seating of the Assembly in the present Salle des Séances in 1832, the Palais-Bourbon served a variety of purposes. Built between 1722 and 1728 for the beautiful and vivacious Louise-Françoise de Bourbon, legitimized daughter of King Louis XIV, the palace resembled a Roman temple outside and contained exquisite parquet floors, mosaics, wood paneling and furniture. Early in the Revolution, the palace was seized by the state and used first as a prison for the king's guards and then as a military storehouse. The National Convention decreed in 1795 that it be turned over to the Council of 500 for an assembly hall, a function that necessitated the destruction of the central apartments to make room for a rotunda. A number of alterations followed. The Roman facade was replaced by a Greek one at Napoleon's order. The Palais-Bourbon of today, at least in outward appearance, is an effective echo of Napoleon's Temple of Glory, the Madeleine, which stands at a distance across the Seine.

• *Admission on application to the National Assembly.*

LES INVALIDES SPREADS A MAZE OF ARCADES AROUND COURTS AND CHAPELS

A MASSIVE ARRAY
OF MARTIAL SPLENDOR

At the head of the Esplanade bordering the Seine is the vast complex of buildings and grounds (*above*) known collectively as Les Invalides (*map, pages 88-89, R-5*). Its main building, the barracks-like Hôtel des Invalides, has been closely linked to French history since Louis XIV commissioned it as a hospital for veterans in 1670. In 1840 Les Invalides was chosen as the site for Napoleon's tomb (*page 94*). Today it houses the greatest museum of its kind in the world, the Musée de l'Armée, whose military displays range from ancient armor to the Armistice bugle of World War I.

● *Open 10-12, 1:30-5 (5:30 in summer); closed Sunday morning and all day Tuesday.*

"VIVE L'EMPEREUR!" is the name of this statue of a member of the Old Guard cheering his emperor. The figure, by Charles Richefeu, is framed by Napoleonic banners in the Sanctuary of Flags of the Musée de l'Armée.

COMPANIONS of Napoleon, mounted figures of his horse "Vizir" and the dog he had in exile on Elba, stand on display in the Musée de l'Armée.

RELICS of Napoleon in the museum include the *bicorne* hat he wore, a cast of his hand and boxed fragments of his first tomb on St. Helena.

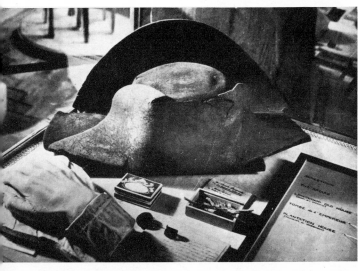

"THE LITTLE CORPORAL," a statue of Napoleon by Charles-Marie-Émile Seurre, is silhouetted in a second-story niche above Les Invalides' Court of Honor. Beneath the floodlit dome in the background lies the Emperor's tomb.

A BOLD "N," emblem of Napoleon's reign, remains blazoned upon many buildings in Paris.

THE TOMB of Napoleon rises from a sunken crypt encircled by monuments to his victories.

A GRANITE BED
FOR A CONQUEROR

Under the Dôme des Invalides (*map, pages 88-89, R-7*), an awesome interplay of space and color sets off the tomb where Napoleon Bonaparte, Emperor of France, was buried 40 years after his death in exile. Directly above a circular gallery (*right, top*) soars the crossed vault. Below, in a crypt bathed by cold blue light, is the ruddy sarcophagus, carved of red porphyry, the funeral stone of Roman emperors. Ten marble bas-reliefs around the crypt celebrate the Emperor's accomplishments—among them, the Code Napoléon, which forms the basis of French law today. Amid these tributes, as the American novelist Henry Miller has written, Napoleon "sleeps soundly in his granite bed."
● *Open 10-12, 1:30-5 (5:30 in summer) every day but holidays.*

THE MAGNIFICENT FOLLY
OF A MAN OF STEEL

Cries of outrage greeted Gustave Eiffel's tower (*map, pages 88-89, K-5*), being built on the Seine to advertise France's new steel industry and to attract tourists to the Paris Exposition of 1889. From 300 noted Parisians came a bitter attack on "that loathsome tin construction." Author Guy de Maupassant went into exile in protest against "this tall, lanky pyramid, this assemblage of iron ladders."

But the tower kept growing (*below*), defying predictions that it would collapse. For engineer Eiffel knew steel. He

GUSTAVE EIFFEL

THE TOWER'S BASE is completed (*left*) after a year's work. This was in January 1888. By April its four pillars (*right*) emerged at a slant from the first platform.

had used it in a great Paris department store and had spun it into bridges on three continents. Experience had taught him so well that in March 1889 he brought the tower to its full 984 feet without repositioning one of 2.5 million rivets.

The tower quickly earned its cost in paid admissions. Artists began discovering its geometric beauty, and a poet called it "a stairway leading to Infinity." Now, from the top of that stairway, over a million visitors a year see spread out below them the panorama shown on the following pages.

THE SHAFT rises (*right*) from the tower's second platform. This was in September 1888. Le Trocadéro, an exposition hall razed in 1936, is framed by the arch.

97

1 ÉCOLE MILITAIRE   3 UNESCO
2 CHAMP-DE-MARS
3
1
2

SOUTH

FROM THE TOWER,
360 DEGREES OF PARIS

In clear weather, the Eiffel Tower is *the* place from which to see Paris. Facing southeast on the second platform 377 feet above the Seine, you see the École Militaire at the end of the Champ-de-Mars (*above left*). If you move clockwise around the platform, you will bring into view the Palais de

7 PALAIS DE CHAILLOT   9 ARC DE TRIOMPHE
8 PONT D'IÉNA
NORTH   9
7
8   SEINE

10 MUSÉE NL. D'ART MODERNE   12 SACRÉ-COEUR
11 PASSERELLE DEBILLY
12
10
11

4 PONT MIRABEAU

5 PONT DE GRENELLE   **6 PONT DE BIR-HAKEIM**

4

5

6

EIFFEL TOWER

7 PALAIS DE CHAILLOT

WEST

7

Chaillot (*right*). The panorama below is the semicircle seen as you turn from the Palais de Chaillot (*left*), past the textured domes and steeples of older Paris, back to your starting point (*far right*). As these pictures show, Paris is a low-lying city striped with avenues and dotted with airy parks. But the tall factories are now sharpening its profiles.

● *All platforms open daily at 10, July 1 to September 15. First and second platforms open to midnight, May 1 to September 30. The top platform closes at 6:30. For off-season hours, call Eiffel Tower Offices, SOL 44-13.*

13 GRAND-PALAIS   **15 ÉGLISE STE-CLOTILDE**

14 ÉGLISE DE LA MADELEINE

EAST

13   14   15

16 HÔTEL DES INVALIDES   **1 ÉCOLE MILITAIRE**   **3 UNESCO**

17 PANTHÉON   **2 CHAMP-DE-MARS**

16   17   1   3

2

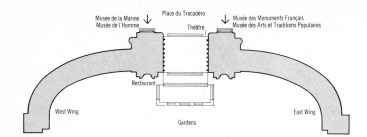

Musée de la Marine ↓
Musée de l'Homme

Place du Trocadéro

Théâtre

↓ Musée des Monuments Français
Musée des Arts et Traditions Populaires

Restaurant

West Wing

East Wing

Gardens

A NAUTICAL PANORAMA, FROM SAIL TO LUXURY LINER

FOUR MUSEUMS plus the large Théâtre National Populaire (*page 178*) are housed in the Palais de Chaillot (*above*). The museums in the west wing are described on these and the following pages. National monuments and French crafts form east-wing displays (*page 187*).

HENRI IV, favorite French king, is carved in wood in one of the fine specimens of figureheads in the Marine Museum. In his reign, 1589-1610, Henri elevated France's maritime prestige by expanding foreign trade and by encouraging the exploration and settlement of Canada.

Although French sea power has been overshadowed by French military deeds, France has a long and spirited maritime history, recapitulated in the Musée de la Marine, probably the finest collection of its kind in the world. Housed in the Palais de Chaillot (*map, pages 88-89, G-2*), the museum traces the development of ships, particularly the French warship and merchantman, from oar through sail to steam. It has dozens of detailed scale models, including ancient galleys; Columbus' *Santa Maria;* a three-decker man-of-war used to teach riggers; a model inlaid with ivory and ebony which took five craftsmen five years to build; the French *Gloire,* which is considered the first steam-driven battleship; and submarines from both world wars. In a gallery of naval paintings and drawings are scenes of the American Revolution, in which French ships were instrumental in breaking Britain's blockade of its rebellious colonies. A collection of instruments illustrates the progress of navigation through the centuries. There are also displays devoted to underwater and polar exploration, fishing boats and small craft.
• *Open 10-5, to 6 on Sundays and in summer; closed Tuesdays.*

TRIM FRIGATE is a model of the 44-gun *La Flore* (*above*), which protected the outposts of the First Empire.

SLEEK LINER *Normandie* is shown in a 25-foot-long model (*below*). The ship burned in New York harbor in 1942.

VIKING-LIKE VESSEL built for Napoleon in 1811 has a statue of Neptune as its figurehead. The barge, over 56 feet long and 11 feet wide, was used only once by the emperor, for an inspection of the port of Antwerp's defenses.

101

A HOME FOR
THE FAMILY OF MAN

The Musée de l'Homme in the Palais de Chaillot is a reflection of French interest in anthropological research. Many of the relics on display here were uncovered in France and rank among the world's oldest, including the skull of a Neanderthal man. Other remarkable exhibits from all over the world document man's most ancient religions, rituals and social developments. Numerous objects came from France's overseas possessions. The collections, covering many ages, cultures and continents, fill 11 large galleries.
• *Open 10-5 daily except Tuesday.*

INTERPRETER of prehistoric cave dwellers' paintings and sculpture, the late Abbé Henri Breuil (*left*) is represented in the Musée de l'Homme by exhibits of the copies he made of cave art.

MAGIC AMULET from the Dordogne region of France (*right*), site of many important discoveries, is thought to have been used by paleolithic hunters to encourage fertility among game.

102

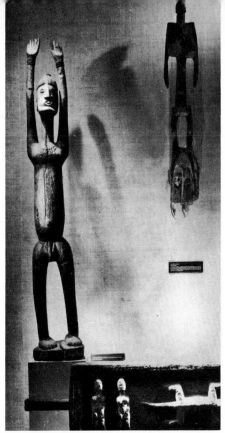

SILK COSTUME embroidered with dragon heads and complete with beard is part of the collection on the Chinese theater in the large Asian section.

ANCESTOR FIGURE, with upstretched arms asking the sky for rain, dominates a display of ceremonial wood carvings by the Dogon tribe of West Africa.

AZTEC STATUE of the god Quetzalcoatl, in the form of a plumed serpent, revolves on a turntable so that visitors can inspect all its intricate sculpture.

103

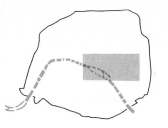

4

CABBAGES
AND
KINGS

The Marais, to the north of the river on the map at left, sprawls from the Palais-Royal, once the domain of nobles, through the markets of Les Halles and into the maze of cul-de-sacs and streets that lead to the Place de la Bastille. This section has repeatedly sent Frenchmen and Frenchwomen storming along the streets to change history. In the Marais are more than 100 magnificent 16th, 17th and 18th Century mansions now become tenements, mustard factories and ironware shops. And the people have changed. Today they are refugees from eastern Europe, Africa and Asia. But when trouble arises, the descendants of the Parisians of 1789 come marching back from the suburbs to appear right here.

HIGHLIGHTS shown in red (*left*) are covered in detail in the following pages; other points of interest in this area appear in black.

105

PEACEFUL GARDENS WITH A RIOTOUS PAST

Although Louis XIV is said to have fallen into one of its fountains as a boy, and its name, Palais-Royal, means royal palace, this collection of somber buildings (*map, pages 104-105, B-2*) with echoing galleries, formal gardens and ghostly statues has been closer to revolutions than to royalty. Cardinal Richelieu built the original unit in 1635 and installed in it his priceless art collection, his household

of some 1,200 and a theater where Molière later appeared. After Richelieu died, the Palais-Royal fell to a series of royal relatives, who made it a center of wit and debauchery, a favorite rendezvous for fashionable rakes, mistresses, dancing girls and duchesses. One noble added the three vast wings that seal off the gardens and, to make ends meet, rented space to gambling houses (the most renowned

A SILENT OASIS in the heart of the city, the grounds of the Palais-Royal were once enlivened by money-changers, artists, circuses, orchestras, even a balloon ascension.

NOVELIST Colette was a loved resident of the Palais-Royal. From her bed near a window overlooking its gardens, she scrutinized the life below and wrote of it in a wry manner.

was at No. 13) and to small shops. Revolutionaries gathered there, and at No. 177 Charlotte Corday bought the knife that stabbed revolutionist Marat in his bathtub. The buildings have since been looted, and gutted by fire and rebuilt. In recent years, the Palais-Royal enclosure has been a preferred address for writers. Colette (*right*), the author of *Gigi* and *Chéri*, spent her last years at 9 Rue de Beaujolais.

A ROYAL SETTING
FOR CLASSIC THEATER

Descended from the royal players who supplied *divertisse-ments* for the court of Louis XIV, the Comédie Française now uses the Salle Richelieu adjoining the Palais-Royal (*map, pages 104-105, B-2*). A Parisian fixture since 1680, it has housed some of the greatest names in French theater.

THE OLD COMÉDIE is shown in an 18th Century print. The players are peeping out at the audience in the Théâtre Royal, which the Comédie occupied from 1689 to 1770. The theater seated 1,500 and was considered one of the most beautiful of its period.

CURTAIN CALL brings elegantly costumed players of the Comédie Française together (*right*) at the end of a recent performance of Corneille's tragedy, *La Mort de Pompée*. Under a 1680 rule, the actors' shares in the receipts depend on seniority.

Although the Comédie is technically responsible to the Ministry of Cultural Affairs, it still erupts with fine bursts of histrionic temperament and to this day stories of backstage quarrels and policy feuds are front page news for the papers, followed as avidly by Parisians as bicycle races. Except for brief interruptions caused by fire, war and revolution, the Comédie, with its repertory of 17th Century French classics in impeccable diction, has been a guardian of French theater and the French language ever since it was founded.

● *For details on performances, see pages 178-179.*

THE LATE, LATE SHOW
AT THE CENTRAL MARKETS

AT 4:30 A.M., an hour after opening time for the fruit and vegetable pavilion (*left*), glaring light and somber shadow engulf trucks, Les Halles workers and customers.

A MOUNTING DISPUTE over the price of fish irritates Charles Allard (*right*) of the Mont Blanc restaurant, who has shopped here for years. Old friends, the two men embraced on meeting but parted in momentary anger without a sale.

Before the last curtain has lowered at the Comédie Française, a few blocks away an earthy melodrama has started in Les Halles (*map, pages 104-105, F-3*), the wholesale food market that caters to the buyers for all the city's stores and restaurants. Trucks stall traffic as far away as a mile. The byways off the Palais-Royal resound with the heave-ho cries of *les forts*, members of France's last functioning medieval guild. Steer carcasses hang outside the church of St-Eustache and mounds of vegetables line the sidewalks. The ordered tumult overwhelms Les Halles until dawn.

The market covers 10 acres at the city's center—overflowing 12 market pavilions, 10 of them built a century ago. The 800-year-old market causes so much congestion and its ancient practices are so costly that the government has vowed to move it to a suburban area after the mid-60s. But considering prior survivals, tourists may be sure of finding Les Halles in full swing—as on these pages—for some time to come. What novelist Émile Zola called "the belly of Paris" may purge itself and, once again, escape what patrons call "the tragedy" of moving to the suburbs.

A SATISFIED SHOPPER, restaurateur Allard examines venison at the stall of another friend (*above*). By 8:00 a.m. (*right*), his purchases completed, he and his assistant (pushing handcart) depart after a morning of marketing.

THE ROBUST CAST
OF A NIGHTLY SPECTACLE

A "FORT" BRINGING IN A CUT OF BEEF

A FISHMONGER RULING HER STALL

A VEGETABLE VENDOR OPENING SHOP

SUPPLIERS of a city, vendor and porters work from midnight, when the first of the food trucks unload, to morning, when the food stalls shut down. Closed only on Sundays, the market may draw up to 20,000 on weekday nights. Émile Zola describes the market workers of his time as having "ribald inflections of the voice and swelling throats." They still have

TRADITIONAL BREAK of onion soup and wine fortifies workers at one of many all-night restaurants. At rear tables, tourists who have come to see the market enjoy a late meal.

A BALANCING ACT WITH CRATES

COMPLETION of the old Hôtel de Ville is celebrated with a great bonfire (*left*). Begun in 1533, the handsome building burned to the ground in 1871.

LIBERATION of Paris is commemorated in 1947 by thousands in front of the Hôtel de Ville (*right*). The present structure dates from 1882.

TEMPLE OF ORDER, CRADLE OF REVOLUTION

The Hôtel de Ville (*map, pages 104-105, H-6*) houses the administration of Paris and the offices of the Préfecture of the Seine. (An *hôtel* was originally a large town house; it is a term now often used for public buildings. Hôtel de Ville means city hall.) The Hôtel is a mecca of rubber stamps and carbon copies. But its history and that of the square on which it stands are anything but mundane. Called the cradle of revolution, it has seen many great and violent events. Robespierre was wounded there during the French Revolution. There was street fighting there during the Revolution of 1848, in the riots following the Franco-Prussian War and, most recently, during the Liberation of Paris in 1944.
● *Admission on application to Syndic Conseil Municipal.*

BATTLING PARISIANS at the Place de l'Hôtel de Ville flatten themselves to avoid German snipers' bullets during the bloody street fighting in August 1944. The Hôtel itself was a Resistance headquarters during the struggle for Paris.

115

AN ANTIQUE JEWEL
CARVED OUT OF A SWAMP

To enter the Place des Vosges (*map, pages 104-105, O-7*) is to step directly into the 17th Century. It was built by Henri IV on what had been river swampland, or *marais*. He built two large pavilions for himself and his queen, and persuaded wealthy nobles to build others according to his master plan. The Place Royale, as it was then called, became an elite address of his century, and it also served as a park and gathering place. It was renamed Place des Vosges for the first department to pay taxes to the republican government in 1800. Nearly every address on the Place des Vosges recalls an illustrious name. Cardinal Richelieu lived at No. 21; Victor Hugo lived at No. 6, in what is now the Musée Victor Hugo.

A PRECISE GRACE still marks the Place des Vosges today (*left*). In the very center, surrounded by a leafy park, stands a statue of Louis XIII. An arcade runs through the rose colored buildings all around the square.

THE GALA OPENING of the square in 1612 (*opposite*), a brilliant affair, features a gigantic equestrian ballet, staged to the music of 150 instruments and cannon fire provided by the garrison at the nearby Bastille.

A WALK AMID
THE MANSIONS OF THE POOR

The two-hour walk mapped at right takes a visitor through the heart of the Marais. This ancient quarter, so lavishly praised by connoisseurs of Paris but so seldom visited by tourists, surprises the eye with beauty and squalor at every glance. In grimy streets and blind alleys rise scores of magnificent *hôtels*—mansions created by great French architects for noble clients. Today, behind broken turrets and colonnades, the dilapidated wings teem with poor workers from three continents, and the once splendid courtyards issue a steady stream of cheap metal and leather goods.

The Marais became a center of fashion and culture in the 17th Century. Its decay began with the Revolution when the emptied mansions of the aristocrats were divided into family apartments. The 19th Century brought to the quarter small industries and many immigrants, and with them poverty and neglect. Recently, several mansions have been restored by public funds to their former elegance, and at night in July and August floodlights turn them into fabulous stage-sets. But by night or day the quarter is rewarding for the insight it offers into the ageless vitality of Paris.

1 Heading east on Rue des Francs-Bourgeois, you see, through two porticoes and across a magnificent court, the colonnaded central facade of the Hôtel de Soubise, the huge main building of the Archives Nationales (*pages 187-188*). An enormous collection of French historical documents has been housed in the rococo palace since 1808.

2 Around the corner is the Hôtel de Rohan at 87 Rue Vieille-du-Temple. This mansion is occasionally used for official balls and soirees.

3 Take two right turns to 5 Rue de Thorigny, the 17th Century Hôtel Aubert de Fontenay. This sumptuous mansion, which now houses a crafts school, is one of the few in the Marais to welcome visitors, and the fine staircase and carvings by Desjardins should certainly be seen.

4 On Rue des Francs-Bourgeois again, walk past the renovated Hôtel Lamoignon, built in the 1580s for a daughter of Henri II. In 1658 it became the home of president of parliament Lamoignon and a meeting place for writers Racine and Boileau.

5 Proceed to the Arcade Nazareth, the superb grilled gateway to the Carnavalet gardens. A left turn just beyond brings you to the famed Musée Carnavalet, where Madame de Sévigné lived and wrote hundreds of remarkable letters that chronicle social life between 1669 and 1695. Today this masterpiece of Renaissance architecture houses a fascinating museum. Lively displays in 79 rooms trace the history of Paris in scale models of the quarters, in clothes and useful articles. Open every day except Tuesday from 10 to 12 and from 2 to at least 5.

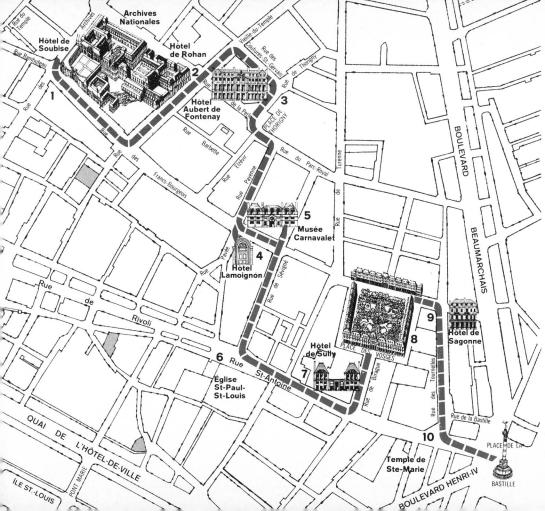

6 On the Rue St-Antoine, there is usually a noisy polyglot throng of shoppers that flows down a row of busy markets and pushcarts. Across the ancient main thoroughfare, near the site of the 17th Century Church of St-Paul-St-Louis, Henri II was wounded mortally in 1559 in a joust.

7 At 62 Rue St-Antoine is the Hôtel de Sully, its courtyard adorned with statuary representing the elements and seasons. Since 1954 this mansion has been under restoration for use as a public building.

8 The route on the map leads to the Place des Vosges (*pages 116-117*) and through its vast arcaded courtyard.

9 Make a right turn to the Hôtel de Sagonne at 28 Rue des Tournelles. This *hôtel* and the one at No. 56 are linked in historical gossip with Ninon de Lenclos, a witty and beautiful 17th Century courtesan whose glittering salon kept her supplied with distinguished lovers.

10 Return to Rue St-Antoine. At No. 17 is the Temple de Ste-Marie, a little Protestant chapel in the charming remnants of a Catholic convent. Just beyond, the walk ends in the Place de la Bastille (*following pages*).

119

THE BIRTHPLACE
OF THE REVOLUTION

If it bore any other name, the busy Place de la Bastille of today (*map, pages 104-105, P-8*) would be just another Paris square. But the associations are inescapable. For this is the birthplace of the French Revolution, which produced modern France and influenced and shaped governments all over the world. Here on July 14, 1789, an angry mob, brought to the breaking point by abuses of the nobility and clergy, attacked the Bastille, a gloomy, high-walled fortress and prison which also served as an arms depot, in the hope of finding ammunition inside. The battle raged about five hours, and when Louis XVI heard of the Bastille's fall, he said, "This is revolt." "No, sire," said the duke who brought the news, "this is revolution." The next day a thousand men began razing this most detested stronghold of absolutism, into whose cells had been thrown, often without trial, men who criticized the king or persons in power. The following year, after the last stone had been carted away, jubilant Frenchmen danced on the site. Reproductions of paintings and prints on the following pages show other dramatic events in and around Paris during the 10-year Revolution.

ASSAULT on the Bastille is depicted at the left. The anniversary of its fall is France's biggest holiday. But though great political significance is attached to the attack, only seven prisoners, all nonpolitical, were freed by the mob.

DEMONSTRATION on May Day by Communists usually is in the Place de la Bastille, at right. Louis-Philippe erected the 169-foot column; it honors the victims of the Parisian rebellions of 1830 and 1848. Some were killed here.

121

THE TWILIGHT OF A MILLENNIUM OF MONARCHY

France set out on the road to the Bastille, and to revolution, in June 1789 in Versailles, where members of the Third (or commoners) Estate defied the throne, the First Estate (the nobles) and the Second (the clergy) by voting to constitute themselves a National Assembly. Three days later, on a side street outside the palace, in a barnlike building once devoted to tennis, they took the bold Tennis Court Oath never to disband until they had given France a constitution. They later declared sacred man's inalienable right to liberty, property and security. But power passed into the hands of the Jacobins and the Girondists, the principal political factions in Paris. By October, when a mob led by a formidable phalanx of market women from Les Halles marched on Versailles and forced the king, queen and National Assembly back to Paris, the French Revolution had at last moved out onto its proper stage. In Paris, where it had flourished, the more than 1,000-year-old monarchy would die. In Paris most of the revolutionaries too would die by their own guillotine—leaving behind a legacy of ideas that still separate Frenchmen into bitterly antagonistic camps.

OATH-TAKING by the Third Estate in the Tennis Court is shown (*opposite*) in an engraving by David. The man reading the oath (*center*) is astronomer Jean Bailly, who served as president of the National Assembly.

THE ROYAL FAMILY, under a Revolutionary guard, comes back to the capital (*right*). The carriage is crossing the Place Louis XV (now the Place de la Concorde), where the king and his queen were beheaded in 1793.

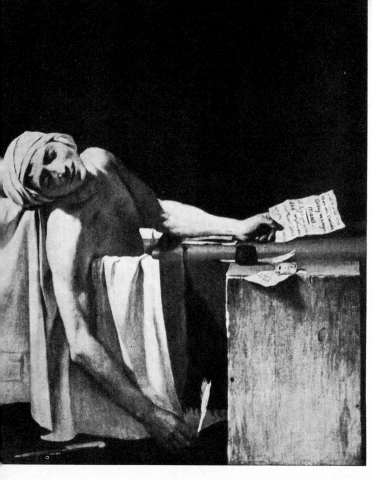

THE PARIS OF
TERROR AND EXULTATION

The Revolution that started as a crusade for the rights of "liberty, property, security and resistance to oppression" soon fell victim to its zealots, and Paris turned red with blood. "Terror," said Robespierre, who controlled the dread Committee of Public Safety, "is only justice . . . more vigorous, more inexorable and therefore Virtue's child." During the Reign of Terror from 1793 to 1794, perhaps as many as 20,000 citizens were executed. When the Revolution turned against Robespierre, his was one of the last heads to fall.

DEATH of Marat, the Jacobin, in his bath (*left*), was painted by David. The fanatic demagoguery of this "friend of the people" roused *Girondiste* Charlotte Corday to stab him.

EXECUTION of Queen Marie Antoinette, then 38 years old, was only one of thousands that took place in 1793 and 1794. David sketched Marie on her way to the guillotine.

BURNING OF ARISTOCRATIC COATS OF ARMS AND FLAGS ON AUGUST 14, 1793, ON THE CHAMP-DE-MARS IS CHEERED BY A NOISY, HAT-WAVING MOB OF PARISIANS

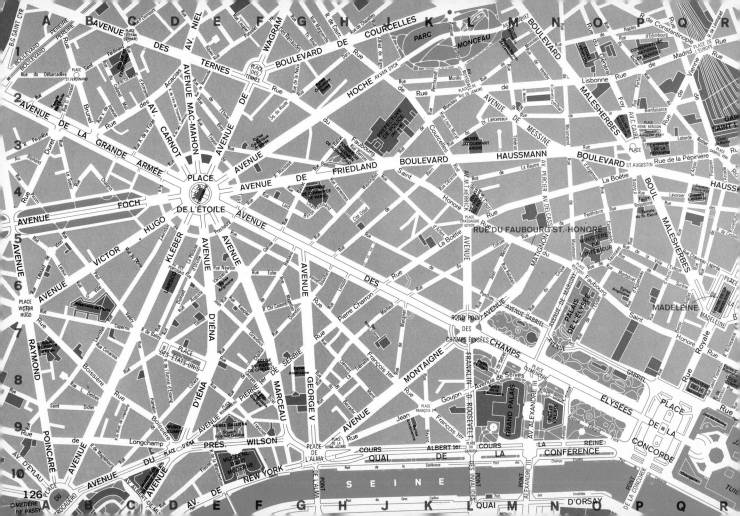

THE BUSTLING CENTER

The human spectacle of Paris, busily getting and spending, swirls around the classically severe Madeleine, the exuberantly robust Opéra and the regally symmetrical Place Vendôme. Against a backdrop of tree-lined boulevards, flashing traffic and glittering stores surges a crowd of shoppers, office clerks, movie-goers, newspaper vendors, would-be *boulevardiers* and just plain people out for a good time. "There are so many things, so many things, so many things to see" goes a Parisian song about a worker from a factory district strutting through the center of town. Despite the throngs and the proliferation of souvenir shops, the area manages to retain much of the high style bestowed by its planners.

HIGHLIGHTS shown in red (*left*) are covered in detail in the following pages; other points of interest in this area appear in black.

MOST FASHIONABLE CHURCH, the Madeleine (*above*) is famous for weddings and funerals. During its 78 years of construction, various proposals were made for its use, including a soldiers' memorial and a railroad terminal.

THE HEADY WORLD
OF THE SHOPPERS' PARIS

The French excel in many ways and certainly in the cultivation of shoppers. Brooding over the area dedicated to buying and spending is the Madeleine (*map, pages 126-127, R-6*), a church in the form of a Greek temple (*left*), dedicated to St. Mary Magdalene. From this church eastward is the world of theaters, cafés and restaurants of 19th Century Paris, clustered on the *grands boulevards*. Here, too, shrewd merchants created department stores, perfected the art of decorating store windows and developed the subtle use of a cup of rich hot chocolate to revive the flagging financial courage of a young housewife dazzled by the profusion of beautiful wares. Today a middle-class Paris pushes up from the *Métro* or climbs down from the buses to storm the historic stores, no longer quite so chic or leisured: the Printemps, harried but still proud of its air of gilded elegance; the Galeries Lafayette, crowded but looking, as ever, like an ornate bird cage; and many others, smaller but just as seductively stocked. No better way exists for a look at what beguiles a Frenchwoman than to stroll through these stores, if you can keep a firm grip on your own susceptibilities.

ROCOCO INTERIOR of the Galeries Lafayette (*left*) looks like the nearby Opéra in decor. Most shops in the area date from the 1850-1870 era.

RUSH HOUR finds Parisians, nearly all shoppers, jamming the stairs at Havre-Caumartin *Métro* station (*right*) outside of the Printemps store.

BARGAINS are advertised in bright lights at the Galeries Lafayette (*below*). Street traffic is heavy and the crowds also buy at sidewalk stands.

THE SPLENDID VISTAS
OF A FORCEFUL BARON

The elegant, vista-filled Paris we know is the work of Baron Georges Eugène Haussmann, Prefect of the Department of the Seine during nearly two decades ending in 1870. He was a daring man with grandiose ideas, and before his fellow citizens could stop him he had taken the town apart and put it together again in his own way. There was no part of Paris Baron Haussmann failed to touch. He found a Paris full of narrow crooked streets, charming courts and no sewers. He left a splendid city of great squares and wide boulevards down which he thought a cannon shot or two would curb all civic turbulence; it also boasted sewers. One of his boulevards bears his name (*map, pages 126-127, S-4*).

FAMOUS CORNER known the world over is at the Boulevard des Capucines and the Rue Auber, near the Opéra (*left*). This site of the Café de la Paix is where Americans have been meeting ever since Haussmann finished remaking the city. If you sit here long enough, they say, all of your friends will pass by.

HAUSSMANN'S WORK is recorded in a print (*above*) showing one of his wrecking crews leveling buildings. Antiquarians bitterly objected but Haussmann went on to build grand thoroughfares like the Avenue de l'Opéra (*right*).

131

A GRANDLY PLUSH SETTING FOR GRAND OPERA

As ornate as a wedding cake, the home of grand opera fills almost three acres on one side of Place de l'Opéra (*map, pages 126-127, T-5*), rising in marbled splendor to an emerald roof 210 feet high. It opened with pomp on January 4, 1875, after 13 years in construction and brief service as a warehouse during the wartime siege of Paris in 1870. Its lavish architecture and décor amused some critics but were good examples of the baroque style popular at the time. The performances made up in tricky scenery and elegant ballet for what they sometimes lacked in musical distinction.

The Opéra devotes so much room to cavernous foyers and great staircases that the auditorium proper, gold and red plush five tiers high, seats only 2,200. It also houses an opera museum and a school for little ballerinas—*les petits rats de l'Opéra*, whom Degas painted with such affection.
- *For details about performances see pages 178-179.*

COMPLEX INTERIOR of the Paris Opéra is detailed in this print, made in 1875 when the building was opened. The only important alteration since that time has been the addition of a rehearsal hall in the dome.

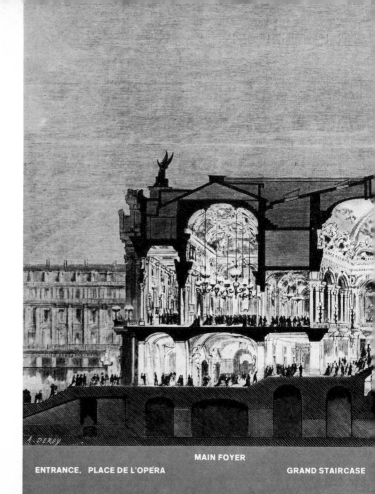

ENTRANCE, PLACE DE L'OPÉRA   MAIN FOYER   GRAND STAIRCASE

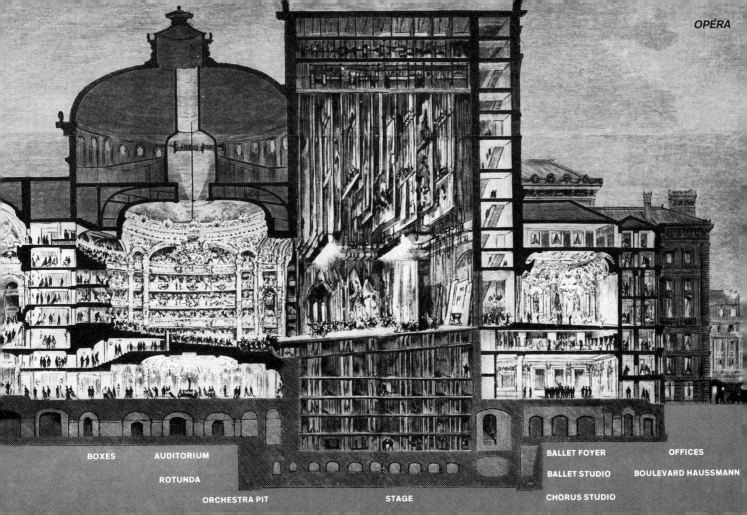

OPÉRA

BOXES   AUDITORIUM

ROTUNDA

ORCHESTRA PIT   STAGE

BALLET FOYER   OFFICES

BALLET STUDIO   BOULEVARD HAUSSMANN

CHORUS STUDIO

SHOWCASE FOR A WORLD OF AFFLUENCE

Admired as a great example of city planning, the 18th Century Place Vendôme is protected against alterations and neon. Around the square are grouped imposing banks, business and government offices, a hotel that has given its name to high living—the Ritz—and, above all, expensive shops.

BOUCHERON, KNOWN FOR JEWELS, HAS CLOTH-OF-GOLD EVENING PURSES: $200

FOR $78 HELLSTERN HAS SLIPPERS DYED TO MATCH HAUTE COUTURE GOWNS

A CHIC SQUARE, Place Vendôme has a column topped by
Napoleon's statue and hon-
oring his army. Torn down
during the revolution of 1871,
the column was rebuilt later.

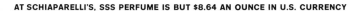

AT SCHIAPARELLI'S, SSS PERFUME IS BUT $8.64 AN OUNCE IN U.S. CURRENCY

AT VAN CLEEF & ARPELS, WORLD-FAMOUS JEWELERS, PRICES GO AS LOW

THE ULTIMATE
IN TASTEFUL EXTRAVAGANCE

The street that lives up to everyone's conception of Parisian luxury is the Rue du Faubourg-St-Honoré (*map, pages 126-127, O-6*). Seductively narrow, it is lined with ancient palaces and rich stores whose proud, firmly established reputations are well deserved. In the early 18th Century, aristocrats used to buy such essentials of life as silks, laces, ribbons and feathers in shops around here, and soon the street became famous for everything from fashions, face patches and collapsible umbrellas to perfume, furniture and dolls. Its tradition of glamor persists in an area that includes the Palais de l'Élysée, the British Embassy, a Dominican convent and a tough training school for policemen.

A stroll down this street past the beautiful displays of all that is new and best in France is bound to bring out the spendthrift strain in the most parsimonious shopper.

● *For details about shops, see pages 180-185.*

FANCY STORE FRONT of Hermès, the 125-year-old leather and silk shop, is a transparent clock face that overlooks the Rue du Faubourg-St-Honoré (*left*). Things bought on this street will always bespeak Paris.

TREASURES for women adorn the window of Lola Prussac (*left*). These accessories are of the exquisite *articles de Paris* variety.

TRADITIONAL SKILL of Hermès' craftsmen, who make all leather goods on the premises, is visible in a saddle and a bag (*right*).

ANTIQUES from the Orient (*below*) are the specialty of Le Dragon Bleu. This display features a collection of Chinese figures.

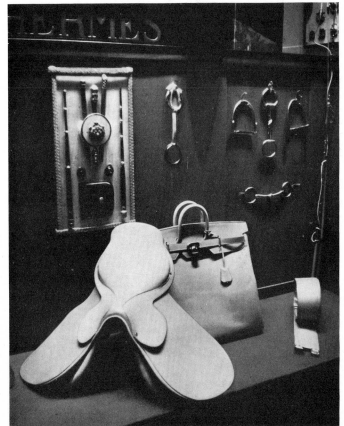

6

THE HEIGHTS AND THE DEPTHS

To many, the brightest face of Paris, shown on the map at left, is Montmartre. This is not only because the top of the hill has sacred connotations or because the streets leading down the hill have been lovingly painted by famous artists; it is mainly because the lower slopes of Montmartre are what people think of when they think of "gay Paree": the cancan, drinking champagne out of slippers and other stimulating pastimes. The area is full of theaters, circuses, street fairs, a few large and exciting night clubs and a multitude of dreary little clip joints. Care is advisable, and care is equally advisable when you go over the hill to rummage for bargains in the Flea Market's shops and stalls.

HIGHLIGHTS shown in red (*left*) are covered in detail in the following pages; other points of interest in this area appear in black.

139

FRENZIED RHYTHMS of Josephine Baker, the American dancer who introduced the Charleston to Paris in the 1920s, are recorded in this poster of her at the Folies Bergère, famous show spot near the *grands boulevards*.

EARTHY FUN
ON THE ROAD TO PIGALLE

North of the *grands boulevards*, Paris offers a variety of entertainment that ranges from the extravaganzas of the Folies Bergère (*left*) and the Casino de Paris, to the sullied ranks of dives clustered around Pig Alley, the G.I.s' contemptuous term for Pigalle. This tawdry district radiates from the Place Pigalle (*map, pages 138-139, F-5*) into dark little streets and alleys. Within it, every device invented to exploit man's loneliness is represented: rows of shady bars and dubious hotels promising various "comforts," all-night movie houses, theaters luridly advertising "permanent strip-tease shows," hot-dog and French-fried potato stands, and penny arcades. Out of the shadows beyond the neon lights leap voices that urge the wide-eyed visitor, in English, German and sometimes French, to enter the most exciting of night clubs where "the nude is revealed in all its splendor like in the Garden of Eden."

The safest or at least the cheapest way to see Pigalle, some say, is on a Paris-by-night tour (*page 25*), but a good way is on foot at twilight, when the workaday world, and the nightworld, heavily made up, jostle good-naturedly.

A GARISH COME-ON lures customers into the Folies Pigalle (*above*). A racy show featuring strip teasers and nude show girls is generally offered here.

SIDEWALK FIRE-EATER does his act regularly at the Place Pigalle. He drinks kerosene (*right*), which he lights with his torch. Afterward he passes the hat.

THE LINGERING MAGIC
OF MONTMARTRE

Above the year-round carnival atmosphere of Pigalle (*pages 140-141*) rises the hilltop enclave of Montmartre, whose name evokes the gay life of Parisian artists and models. The image of Montmartre is largely the creation of late 19th Century painters like Manet, Renoir, Toulouse-Lautrec and Degas, who lived there, worked there and waged tumultuous discussions in café-dance halls like the Moulin de la Galette (*right*). Most of all, the world's vision of Montmartre arises from Maurice Utrillo's paintings of pale streets, narrow stairways and hidden squares. The five Utrillo paintings seen here and on the following pages, with photographs of the actual sites today, show how the artist transmuted reality.

In medieval times a rowdy wayside village on the road to Paris, Montmartre had settled into bucolic drowsiness long before its discovery by 19th Century artists. *Galettes* (griddle cakes), sold by millers' wives, gave their name to one of the district's most famous windmills. Today much of Montmartre looks like a tawdry stage-set imitation of its romantic past. But a stroll through the twisting back streets at odd hours can recapture fleeting glimpses of the lingering magic.

A DANCE HALL, the Moulin de la Galette, at the junction of Rue Lepic and Rue Girardon, is viewed (*above*) as Utrillo saw and painted it in 1933 and (*right*) as it appears today. It boasts the last of the many windmills that used to grind the flour for the village.

A STREET SCENE depicted by Utrillo on the Avenue Junot when he lived there is shown at left; how it looks now is seen below. Appalled by the changes in Montmartre, Utrillo scrawled a bitter poem on his canvas lamenting the vulgarity overtaking the village.

CHANGING SCENES
AND UNCHANGING ART

A CHARMING SQUARE, Place Charles Dullin (*below*) is little changed since Utrillo painted its Théâtre Montmartre (*left*). Now known as the Théâtre de l'Atelier, its stage is famed for avant-garde productions between the two world wars.

STEEP HILLS make some Montmartre streets impassable to wheeled traffic—hence the stairways like the one seen in Utrillo's *Impasse Cottin* (*left*). The artist found the stairs picturesque and so will hardy explorers, but for Parisians dwelling on the heights these climbs (*below*) are merely a direct way home.

A SERENE SQUARE as Utrillo painted it (*above*), the Place du Tertre (*right*) has become a bustling, noisy and commercialized tourist attraction. In summer it is crowded with restaurant tables, umbrellas, hawkers, and painters who beseech diners to let them catch their likenesses at the table.

THE HILL OF MARTYRS
AND SINNERS

For eight decades the great white basilica of Sacré-Coeur (*center, right*) has brooded on its high hill over Montmartre. The shrine was built as an act of national atonement after the French defeat by the Prussians in 1871. The hill itself was made holy by the martyrdom of St. Denis, first Bishop of Paris, who is supposed to have been beheaded here in the Third Century. Here, in the 12th Century, gentle Benedictines chanted lauds and matins about three blocks away from the place where lusty old Aristide Bruant, who wrote the songs Utrillo's Paris sang, lifted a husky voice in praise of *Nini, the Dog-Skinned Girl*. La Goulue and Jane Avril, the "little friends" painted by Toulouse-Lautrec, danced their lives away on these slopes, and many foreign armies sent against Paris marched over this hill. Now a visitor can lean upon the white balustrade of Sacré-Coeur or climb up high into the basilica's dome and look down on 2,000 years of history.

SACRED HEART SHRINE tops the Butte de Montmartre (Heights of Montmartre) with its gleaming white dome. Imposing stairways and a funicular railway lead to Sacré-Coeur, which seats a congregation of 9,000.

SEARCHING FOR BARGAINS, VISITORS INSPECT AN ARRAY OF BRIC-A-BRAC IN A FLEA MARKET SHOP. THE FAMOUS MARKET EXUDES AN AIR OF SEEDY PROSPERITY

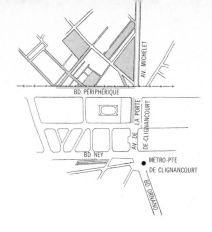

THE FLEA MARKET, its covered areas shaded in gray (*left*), blankets some 48 acres. Its *Métro* station, the Porte de Clignancourt, is a 30-minute ride from the center of Paris.

PORTLY OWNER of a Flea Market shop (*right*) relaxes between customers. Like most dealers today, he knows the value of his wares and can afford to wait for his price.

A JUMBLED ATTIC
OF TREASURE AND TRASH

Everything portable, from secondhand tools to antiques and furniture, can be bought in the Flea Market, open for business or haggling from 7 a.m. to 7 p.m. on Saturdays, Sundays and Mondays. Named after the wild life in its cut-rate bedding, the market began about 1892, when police herded itinerant peddlers onto the prairie of St-Ouen, just north of the city. The crude encampment grew into a jumble of flimsy shops, covered stalls and sidewalk displays. Scoured by dealers, the market is fun to explore, short on bargains. (See pages 180-185 for other open-air markets and fairs.)

FLEA MARKET

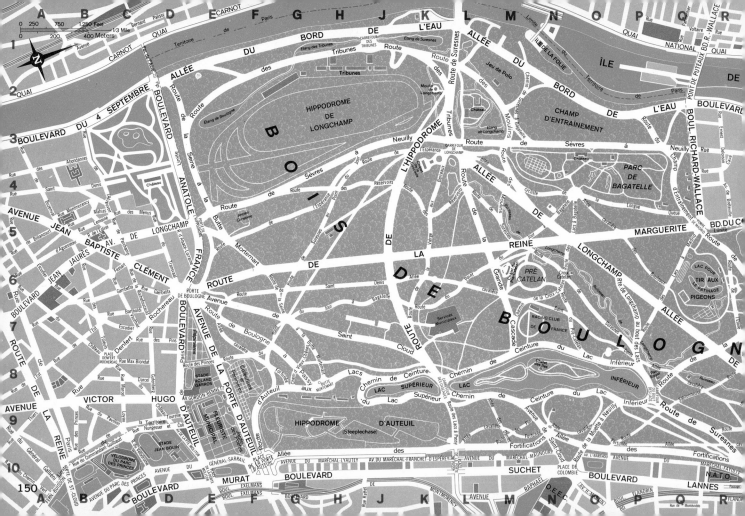

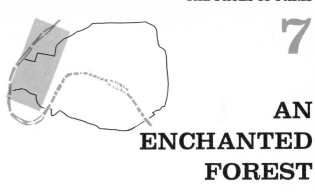

7

AN
ENCHANTED
FOREST

Take a 2,500-acre confusion of green lawns, formal gardens, a tiny château, winding trails, waterfalls, brooks, bridle paths, race tracks and two lakes. Add an amusement park for children, delightful restaurants and an outdoor theater and you have the Bois de Boulogne (mapped at left), a marvelous wooded breathing space running from the western edge of Paris to a winding loop in the Seine below the cliffs of St-Cloud. Le Bois, as Parisians call their enchanted forest, was once the hunting preserve of kings and has been a smart place to be seen since the 17th Century. Napoleon III gave it to the city in 1852 and Baron Haussmann—that indefatigable remaker of Paris—gave it the look it has today.

HIGHLIGHTS of the Bois de Boulogne are shown on this map (*left*) and are described in detail in the pages of the guide which follow.

AN INFINITE VARIETY OF PASTORAL PLEASURES

The Bois de Boulogne is a trip to the country completely within the city limits. Trees grow there in such profusion that roads are hidden from one another, and each step in the Bois leads to some new surprise. There are open fields for soccer players (*le football* to the French); paths for hikers, cyclists and horseback riders (*right*); lakes for boaters (*left*); meadows and clearings for picnickers; grassy banks by the Seine for sunning; quiet tree-shaded alleys for people who like to wash and polish their cars. For the greatest of all French pastoral (and urban) pleasures, eating, there are luxurious restaurants like Pré Catelan where one can eat at tables under the trees by a quiet pond, or under the stars in the Pavillon Dauphine at tables by a dance floor, or in the sun at tables on a terrace near the waterfall at Pavillon de la Cascade. And in the trackless stretches of wilderness beyond that, a dog may run without a leash.

BOATING ON THE GRAND LAC catches the nostalgic spirit of Sunday afternoons in the Bois de Boulogne (*left*). An island in the lake's center has an outdoor restaurant where weary boaters can stop for tea.

A MISTY MORNING IN THE BOIS makes its shaded bridle paths (*opposite*) seem hundreds of miles from the city. Even taxi drivers have been known to get lost in the twisting roads wandering through the Bois.

TOP HATS and elegant dress (*left*) are a hallmark of the closing race of La Grande Semaine, annual feature at the Longchamp track, one of two race courses in the Bois.

TINY CHÂTEAU, built in 64 days to win a bet, is hidden (*right*) in the formal gardens of the Parc de Bagatelle. Its spring flower displays, especially its roses, are famous.

FOR THE ELEGANT WORLD AND

There are those who will not respond to the Bois de Boulogne's simple and bucolic enticements. For these sophisticates, the Bois reserves its ultimate weapon: two splendid race courses. At the Hippodrome de Longchamp, the Grand Prix de Paris, a major horse race and social event, marks the end of the late spring season. For those who prefer the

EXCITING RIDES on merry-go-rounds make the Jardin d'Acclimatation (*right*)—part zoo, part amusement park —the children's favorite corner of the Bois de Boulogne.

THE YOUNG IN HEART

steeplechase, there is the Champ de Courses d'Auteuil. For children, the Bois de Boulogne provides all the fun of a day at a country fair. First, there is its miniature railway leading from the Porte Maillot to the Jardin d'Acclimatation, then the animals in the zoo and the rides. And if all these attractions pall, they can fly kites in the neighboring fields.

RECURRING EVENTS
IN THE PARIS YEAR

Paris packs its year with fairs, fêtes, sports events, art exhibitions and holidays. Some of the best of these events, recurring at fixed times annually, are listed below.

January

HOLIDAY New Year's Day, when people wish each other *"bonne année, bonne santé"*–a good year of good health. **FÊTE** Day of the Three Kings, January 6, when children hunt for tiny beans in their cake which make them king for the day. **THEATER** Important openings. **MUSIC** Sunday afternoon concerts by the Concerts Pasdeloup (Palais de Chaillot until April) and Concerts Lamoureux (Salle Pleyel all year).

February

THEATER AND ART The season is now in full spate.

March

FÊTE Mardi gras, sometimes in February, features parties at home in masks and costumes. **FLOWER SHOW** Masses of tulips in the Parc de Bagatelle; this runs into April. **EXHIBITION** Salon des Arts Ménagers (household arts) at the Palais de la Défense, a display of stoves and freezers plus incredible kitchen gadgetry. The Salon also offers an unlimited opportunity to sample, with no charge, French wines and sauces.

April

HOLIDAYS *Pâques* (Easter Sunday, often in March) is the occasion for magnificent music in the churches, chocolate eggs for good children. Easter Monday. **ART** Salon des Indépendants at the Grand-Palais, a vast viewing of current painting. **EXHIBITIONS** Foire aux Jambons near the Place de la Bastille, dating back to 1222, salutes all the famous hams of France and the specialties related to ham–balonies, sausages, pâtés, pigs' feet; sample offerings are generous; this fair sometimes takes place in March. Gingerbread fair near the Place de la Nation has less to do with goodies than with shooting galleries and merry-go-rounds and other entertainment for the passersby.

May

HOLIDAYS May Day pulls all Paris outdoors wearing *muguet* (lilies of the valley), some to march in the political parades and the rest to picnic in the country. Ascension Day. Whitsunday. **EXHIBITION** Yacht show, on the river near the Pont d'Iéna, displays the newest in pleasure craft.

June

FÊTE The last Sunday of the month, when the Grand Prix de Paris is run at Longchamp, ends society's high season. **ILLUMINATION** Notable buildings and public squares, 21 in all, are illuminated nightly through the summer from 9:30 to 11:30 (midnight on Sundays). Sculpture in the Louvre is dramatically lighted every Friday night all year round. "Sound and Light" (*"Son et Lumière"*) spectacles with a voice telling the stories of the châteaux while the lights draw the spectators' eyes to the section being described, start at 9:30 at the great palaces at Versailles and Vincennes. The Napoleonic epic is told at the Invalides.

July

HOLIDAY July 14, Bastille Day, is celebrated with a big military parade on the Champs-Élysées in the morning, fireworks all around the city at night, and in many quarters the people dance in the streets.

August

HOLIDAYS The whole town is *"en vacances"*–many stores and restaurants close down for the month, the city moves at the more leisurely pace of the tourist. Assumption Day, August 15. World War II liberation day–August 24–is marked by the ringing of church bells.

September

FÊTE Montmartre wine festival, sometimes October. **FLOWER SHOW** Dahlias at Parc de Sceaux. **ART EXHIBITS** Private galleries begin reopening after summer. **EXHIBITION** International Marine show on the Seine near Pont d'Iéna.

October

THEATER All state theaters are running, and commercial theaters begin opening new plays. **ART EXHIBIT** Opening of the Salon d'Automne, historically important exhibit at the Grand-Palais. **EXHIBITION** International Automobile show at the Parc des Expositions, Porte de Versailles, jams the town with visitors and makes reservations difficult to come by–the very latest French, American, British, German, Italian, Czechoslovakian, Russian standard cars are on display plus some unusual custom-made automobiles.

November

HOLIDAYS November 1, All Saints' Day. November 11, Armistice Day, is celebrated by a ceremony at the tomb of the Unknown Soldier at the Arc de Triomphe. November 25, St. Catherine's Day, witnesses a parade of the seamstresses along the Avenue Montaigne, each wearing a weird hat run up for the occasion. Social activities of the winter season are now in full swing. **ART EXHIBIT** The Salon d'Hiver opens at the Palais de New York.

December

HOLIDAYS Christmas is a religious feast and family party; after midnight Mass the family walks home for *le réveillon,* a traditional dinner of oysters, *foie gras,* sausages, cakes, candies, pancakes and white wine; for youngsters sent off to bed early, gifts from *Père Noël* are left in their shoes. La nuit du St-Sylvestre (New Year's Eve) is celebrated in romping good cheer in the cafés (reservations must be made long in advance) and with many parties at home.

PART IV A PARIS DIRECTORY
A Key to Eating, Buying, Dancing and Whatnot

On the following pages are concise listings (*indexed at right*) with brief commentaries on almost everything you can buy, see and do in the fabulous bazaar of the spirit and the senses that is Paris.

The preceding section of this guide has highlighted many of the most worth-while points of interest to visitors. But there are numerous other places that a particular individual may want to see or know about; only a listing with a broad range of alternatives can reveal these to him. In this directory are many such places—from theaters and museums to châteaux in the nearby countryside. And, of course, there are the human needs for good shelter and enticing food, covered under the hotel and restaurant categories, with a special section on how to select a meal. Finally, there is the question of when to make your trip to Paris. To help you to reach this decision, information about some of the recurring events that make up the life and rhythm of the city is given in the calendar of annual happenings (*opposite*). Here then is the stuff for planning your stay in detail: suggestions designed to be useful in all aspects of the traveler's daily life.

HOTELS GREAT AND SMALL, DE LUXE AND SIMPLE

Paris hotels range from the luxurious to the simple and inexpensive. The *grand luxe* hotels, most of them centrally located on the Right Bank, offer large, elegant rooms and superb service. The less expensive hotels, mainly on the Left Bank, have smaller rooms and less efficient equipment than the average American motel. The most inexpensive hotels have few rooms with baths. For a short stay in Paris, a convenient expensive hotel is worth while. For a longer stay, a small, inexpensive hotel will save money. A concise but representative selection of hotels by area and cost follows. Quoted price ranges (indicated by symbols explained below) do not include tips or taxes, which can add 15 to 25 per cent to the bill. Almost all hotels, even those without restaurants, serve a French breakfast (*croissant* and coffee) on request.

Hotel French

ROOM SERVICE Please, *S'il vous plaît;* Thank you very much, *Merci bien;* Send the waiter, *Envoyez le garçon;* Serve breakfast at eight o'clock, *Servez-moi le petit déjeuner à huit heures;* Orange juice, rolls and coffee, *Jus d'orange, petits pains et café;* Bacon and eggs, *Oeufs au lard;* Come in, *Entrez;* Wait, *Attendez.*

MAID AND VALET SERVICE Take these dresses (suits) to be cleaned, *Envoyez ces robes (costumes) à nettoyer;* I want it pressed only, *À repasser seulement;* This is to be washed, *Ceci est à laver;* I want it for tonight, *Je le voudrais pour ce soir;* How long will it take? *Combien de temps prendra-t-il?*

Right Bank: Champs-Élysées-Étoile

BELFAST
10 Avenue Carnot (58, D-1) ETO 12-10
†† Good, family-type, located on a broad avenue near the Étoile. It has a restaurant but no bar.

BELLMAN
37 Rue François-I (58, H-4) ELY 62-51
††† On a handsome street handy to the shops and restaurants of the Avenue Montaigne. Heavily patronized by American servicemen. Bar but no restaurant.

CALIFORNIA
16 Rue de Berri (58, J-2) ELY 93-00
††† First-class and modern, much favored by American journalists. Only a few steps from the Champs-Élysées. Restaurant and a good American-style bar.

CELTIC
6 Rue Balzac (58, G-2) BAL 09-25
††† Old-fashioned, residential and quiet, the Celtic is patronized by those eternal travelers, airline pilots. Very near the Étoile end of the Champs-Élysées. Restaurant and bar.

CHÂTEAU FRONTENAC
54 R. Pierre-Charron (58, H-4) ELY 35-07
††† Lively, commercial and first-class, on a busy street that connects the Champs-Élysées with the Avenue George-V. Attractive bar and restaurant.

CLARIDGE
74 A. des Champs-Élysées (58, H-3) ELY 33-01
††† The Claridge is famous and old, with suites overlooking the Champs-Élysées. An attractive feature is its indoor swimming pool. Bar and restaurant. Tea dancing from September to May.

ÉLYSÉE PARK
2 Rue Jean-Mermoz (58, L-4) ELY 31-96
††† Small, distinguished, with a quiet, subdued atmosphere. Near the gardens of the Champs-Élysées. Bar and restaurant service in rooms only.

FARNESE
32 Rue Hamelin (58, C-5) PAS 98-27
†† Small, comfortable, old-fashioned, excellent for families. It is located on a quiet street. Bar and restaurant.

FRANKLIN ROOSEVELT
18 R. Clément-Marot (58, H-4) ELY 75-64
†† Despite its name, this is small and very French, on a quiet side street off the Avenue Montaigne. Convenient to

† *Symbols indicate average daily cost of double room:* † *under 30 NF;* †† *30-60 NF;* ††† *60-100 NF;* †††† *over 100 NF.*

the grand *couturiers*. No bar or restaurant.

GEORGE-V

31 Avenue George-V (58, G-4) BAL 35-30
†††† One of Paris' most luxurious and most famous, the George-V attracts movie stars, moguls and fashion buyers from the top shops. Suites available on application. Lively bar and restaurant.

D'IÉNA

28 Avenue d'Iéna (58, E-6) KLE 07-10
††† Luxurious, and the service is good. It is near the Palais de Chaillot and the river. Bar and restaurant.

LANCASTER

7 Rue de Berri (58, H-2) ELY 90-43
†††† Small, sedate; one of the best of the de luxe class that abounds in the Champs-Élysées area. It is favored by film stars and other important people. Bar and restaurant.

MASSENET

5 bis Rue Massenet (88, C-4) AUT 53-61
†† One of the best of the less expensive hotels on the Right Bank; the Massenet is in the heart of Passy, a modern residential section of Paris, and just off the Rue de Passy, which is noted for its markets and small shops. It has a restaurant but no bar.

NAPOLÉON

40 Av. de Friedland (58, F-1) CAR 74-20
††† Quiet, excellent, situated on a wide, tree-lined boulevard, close to the Étoile, a pleasant walk from the beautiful Parc Monceau. Bar and restaurant.

LA PÉROUSE

40 Rue La Pérouse (58, D-3) PAS 43-68
††† Conservative but stylish, not far from the Étoile, patronized by distinguished guests. It has a good restaurant but it is not to be confused with the famous Lapérouse restaurant which is on the Left Bank. No bar.

PLAZA ATHÉNÉE

25 Avenue Montaigne (58, J-6) BAL 43-30
†††† Luxurious and fronting on a handsome avenue. Both bar and restaurant are good and attract an interesting crowd.

PRINCE DE GALLES

33 Avenue George-V (58, G-4) BAL 39-90
†††† De luxe and similar to its neighbor, the George-V, but less frequented by Americans. Its bar attracts fashionable people and the restaurant is good.

RAPHAËL

17 Avenue Kléber (58, D-3) KLE 07-70
†††† The Raphaël ranks as one of the city's very best. Quiet and sedate with

superb rooms and service. Bar and restaurant.

ROYAL MONCEAU

35 Avenue Hoche (126, H-2) CAR 78-00
††† Near the charming Parc Monceau and its fashionable residential neighborhood, the Royal Monceau has a cozy bar and an inside patio. A quiet and relaxed place.

SAN-REGIS

12 Rue Jean-Goujon (58, K-6) ELY 41-90
††† The San-Regis is fine, small, and has excellent service and pleasant rooms. It is located on one of the most

Right Bank: Concorde—Opéra

AMBASSADOR

16 Bd Haussmann (127, V-5) PRO 63-74
††† A cooperative and friendly management, especially liked by Americans. Tastefully decorated, only a few steps from the Opéra. Hairdressing shop. Bar, restaurant.

ASTOR

11 Rue d'Astorg (126, P-4) ANJ 04-31
†† A reliable, old-fashioned place on a quiet residential street, but near the Rue du Faubourg-St-Honoré. Bar and restaurant.

BEDFORD

17 Rue de l'Arcade (126, R-5) ANJ 40-32

elegant streets in Paris, a short distance from the Seine.

LA TRÉMOILLE

14 R. de La Trémoille (58, H-5) BAL 64-95
††† The beautiful Place de l'Alma and the fashionable Avenue Montaigne are only a few steps away. No bar or restaurant, light meals served in rooms.

WINDSOR-ÉTOILE

14 Rue Beaujon (58, G-1) CAR 73-00
††† First-class, conveniently situated between the Avenue Hoche and the Avenue de Friedland. It attracts airline crews, has a bar and restaurant.

††† The Bedford is quiet and a convenient place to stay in a bustling part of town. It has a bar and restaurant.

BRISTOL

112 Rue du Faubourg-St-Honoré (126, N-5) ELY 23-15
†††† Subdued and luxurious, catering largely to diplomats and voyaging VIPs. It is located on Paris' most fashionable shopping street.

CASTIGLIONE

40 Rue du Fbg-St-Honoré (126, Q-7) ANJ 07-50
††† Near smart shops and the Place Vendôme. Bar and restaurant.

CONTINENTAL

3 Rue de Castiglione (127, S-9) OPE 18-00

†††† Second largest hotel in town. Recent renovations. Some suites overlooking the Tuileries; large bar and restaurant and spacious public rooms. In the heart of central Paris.

CRILLON

10 Place de la Concorde (126, Q-8) ANJ 24-10

†††† Luxurious and famous, the Crillon caters to a steady stream of dignitaries and celebrities. Front rooms have a beautiful view of the Place de la Concorde. Excellent dining room and bars heavily populated with journalists and diplomats.

DUMINY

3 Rue du Mont-Thabor (127, S-9) OPE 33-21

†† Small and quiet, located between the Tuileries Garden and the Place Vendôme. No restaurant or bar.

FRANCE ET CHOISEUL

239 and 241 Rue St-Honoré (127, S-8) OPE 41-92

†† Excellent but small, family-type hotel much favored by European visitors to Paris and by the French. Has an attractive inner court with a garden and tables, a restaurant, but no bar.

GRAND-HOTEL

12 Bd des Capucines (127, S-6) OPE 05-40

††† The largest hotel in all France, the Grand has an ideal location, around the corner from the Opéra and American Express. The Café de la Paix is in the same building. It is only a short stroll from everything else in the center of the city. The hotel has a busy, big city air, but the rooms are pleasant, the lobbies ornate. Bar and restaurant.

LOTTI

7-9-11 Rue de Castiglione (127, S-9) RIC 93-84

††† Luxurious, with a superior restaurant, pleasant small bar. The location is ideal: a few steps take the visitor to the Place Vendôme, the Rue de Rivoli or the Rue du Faubourg-St-Honoré.

MANCHESTER

1 Rue de Gramont (127, V-7) RIC 80-25

† Located about halfway between the Opéra and the Bourse. There is a pleasant touch of green in the small courtyard. Restaurant but no bar.

MÉTROPOLITAIN

8 Rue Cambon and 42 Rue du Mont-Thabor (126, R-8) OPE 61-44

†† Fairly modern. Located near the Tuileries Garden. It has a restaurant and a modest bar.

MEURICE

228 Rue de Rivoli (127, S-9) OPE 32-40

†††† One of the best in Paris. The décor is elaborate, an attractive example of the turn-of-the-century style; service is excellent. A good restaurant and bar. Only the suites with sitting rooms overlook the Tuileries.

HÔTEL DE PARIS

8 Boulevard de la Madeleine (127, S-6) OPE 03-80

††† Large and modern, with all rooms overlooking streets and boulevards (as opposed to courts). Has new restaurant and a lively bar.

RÉGINA

2 Place des Pyramides (127, T-10) OPE 74-00

††† One side of this good, moderate-sized hotel faces on the Tuileries Garden. The reception rooms are stylish but there is no restaurant. Snack and cocktail bars.

RITZ

15 Place Vendôme (127, S-8) OPE 28-30

†††† A great, internationally famous hotel which provides luxury-with-taste for diplomats and nobility and the wealthy of all nations. It has shops, bars, restaurants, a garden and a beautifully trained staff. It is located in the center of everything, only a few steps from Van Cleef and Arpels' jewelry store, Chanel's dress shop and the Morgan and Chase banks. Dogs are accommodated for 9 NF a day.

ST-JAMES ET D'ALBANY

211 Rue St-Honoré and 202 Rue de Rivoli (127, T-9) OPE 02-30

†† Much favored by well-to-do Britons. Some of the rooms face on a pretty interior courtyard and garden, a few on the Rue de Rivoli and the Tuileries; bar, restaurant and parking facilities in the courtyard.

SCRIBE

1 Rue Scribe (127, S-6) OPE 92-70

††† Centrally located, lively and commercial, and old-fashioned in size of rooms and furniture. Its bar and restaurant are well known.

VENDÔME

1 Place Vendôme (127, S-8) OPE 48-24

††† Small, club-like, antique and chic. Rooms are divided into suites. Small restaurant. No bar.

WESTMINSTER

13 Rue de la Paix (127, T-6) OPE 36-40

††† Founded in 1805, it is pleasantly old-fashioned. Many suites with sitting rooms. On a street that connects the Place de l'Opéra and the Place Vendôme. No restaurant or bar.

Left Bank: Latin Quarter— St-Germain-des-Prés—Montparnasse

ANGLETERRE
44 Rue Jacob (26, K-1) LIT 87-91
†† Average but good and close to the Seine and the lively cafés of St-Germain-des-Prés. No bar or restaurant.

CARLTON PALACE
207 Bd Raspail (26, J-10) DAN 62-94
† A rustic old hotel with a friendly management and a mixed French-and-foreign clientele. It is located within easy reach of the Jardin du Luxembourg. No bar or restaurant.

LUTETIA
43 Boulevard Raspail (26, H-4) LIT 44-10
†† Largest on the Left Bank in the heart of the shopping district and convenient to bus and *Métro* lines. Large restaurant and bar, lively public rooms; banquet and conference rooms.

HOTEL DE NICE ET DES BEAUX ARTS
4 bis Rue des Beaux-Arts (26, L-1) DAN 54-05
†† Good, average and family-type, well liked by Europeans and Americans for its French atmosphere and proximity to Left Bank art galleries and Paris' famous Beaux-Arts school. No bar, no restaurant. Free garage.

PAS-DE-CALAIS
59 Rue des Saints-Pères (26, J-2) LIT 78-74
†† In the center of Paris' celebrated Left Bank café life. No bar or restaurant.

SAINTS-PÈRES
65 R. des Saints-Pères (26, J-2) LIT 44-45
†† A favorite of old Paris hands. Near a restaurant-rich area, it has no restaurant or bar of its own.

STUDIO
4 Rue du Vieux-Colombier (26, K-4) LIT 31-81
† This rates as a bargain. Across the street is the impressive Church of St-Sulpice. Some rooms—5 of 37—have baths. No bar, restaurant or elevator.

TRIANON-PALACE
3 Rue de Vaugirard (26, N-5) DAN 88-10
†† Old-fashioned, quiet and near the Jardin du Luxembourg. It is patronized mostly by teachers and students. Bar and restaurant.

URSULINES
12 R. des Ursulines (26, 0-9) ODE 99-82
† Modest and clean. A favorite among American students, who often work as

night receptionists to help pay for their rooms. No bar, restaurant or elevator.

VICTORIA PALACE
6 Rue Blaise-Desgoffe (26, G-7) LIT 80-40

Left Bank: Palais Bourbon

LA BOURDONNAIS
111-113 Avenue de La Bourdonnais (88, 0-7) SOL 45-42
†† Furnished with big armchairs and thick carpets, unpretentious but excellent. Near the École Militaire, it has a charming patio, a restaurant and a bar.

BOURGOGNE ET MONTANA
7 Rue de Bourgogne (89, S-3) INV 20-22
†† The building is old, but the interior has been modernized and there is a pleasant restaurant. The neighborhood is full of government buildings and is very quiet at night.

CAYRE
4 Boulevard Raspail (26, G-2) BAB 10-82
†† Old-fashioned but well-maintained. The service is good and there is a restaurant and bar.

DERBY
5 Avenue Duquesne (88, P-7) INV 12-05
†† The management here is notable for being helpful to a befuddled tourist. *Décor* is plain but clean and agreeable

†† A pleasant lobby, newly renovated rooms and restaurant, and the unusual advantage of its own garage. In a narrow sidestreet on the fringe of the artists' quarters near the Gare Montparnasse. Bar.

and there are both a bar and a restaurant. Across from the École Militaire.

MONTALEMBERT
3 Rue Montalembert (89, W-5) LIT 68-11
†† One of the best on the Left Bank. It is smartly and expensively furnished, has generous-sized rooms and excellent service. Within easy walking distance of St-Germain-des-Prés café life and the Seine. Restaurant and bar.

PONT ROYAL
5-7 Rue Montalembert (89, W-5) LIT 42-50
††† A cheerful lobby, good service and bright rooms. Conveniently situated within a short walk of the Right Bank. It has a restaurant and bar.

QUAI VOLTAIRE
19 Quai Voltaire (89, Y-4) LIT 42-91
†† With luck you may get a room with windows and a little iron balcony overlooking the Seine. The view here, across from the Louvre, is superb. There is a bar but no restaurant.

A CANDID GUIDE
TO THE FOOD OF PARIS

One of the dividends of a Paris visit—your first or your 50th—is the chance to sample what the French insist is the best cuisine in the world. Like the Italians and the Chinese, the French look upon cooking not as a task or a craft, but as an art. They think of their cuisine as a harmonious and scientific blending of superb ingredients, to which seasoning has been subtly added to bring out delicate flavors. However, for tourists, there can be too much of a good thing, resulting in a *crise de foie,* or in English an upset stomach.

This section of the guide offers some basic advice on how to eat and drink in Paris. On pages 162-164, there are brief discussions of the various parts of a French meal—the *hors-d'oeuvre,* meats, fish, fowl, vegetables, cheeses and wines. Next there is a sample menu taken from one of Paris' best restaurants, and guidance on how to read it (*page 165*). This is followed by lists of more than 100 fine restaurants and cafés (*pages 166-173*). There are brief discussions of each restaurant's virtues, with its address, telephone number and price range. All serve food prepared by a chef who approaches his craft with the devotion of an artist.

Hors-d'Oeuvre   In French restaurants these range from the simplest appetizers, such as a sliced tomato in a vinaigrette dressing, to complex works of culinary art. There are thousands of these variations on a theme, using basic ingredients as a starting point. Here are six popular *entrées:*

ARTICHAUT Artichoke, or artichoke hearts, usually served vinaigrette (oil-and-vinegar sauce).

CREVETTES The small shrimp, usually served with a vinaigrette sauce or a mayonnaise.

ESCARGOTS Snails, usually served in their shells with a garlic-and-parsley butter sauce.

LANGOUSTE Rock lobster, frequently prepared hot with various sauces.

MOULES Mussels, usually served cold with a vinaigrette sauce or steamed open in a broth.

PÂTÉ Pâtés range from delicate *pâté de foie gras* (ground goose liver) to *pâté maison,* a hearty chopped-meat specialty of the chef.

Meats   French meats (called *viandes*) of all kinds are excellent—though the cuts are not always recognizable to Americans. No restaurant of any sort ever serves meat that has been frozen, and almost all eating places send men to the market in the early morning to buy whatever looks freshest and juiciest that day. Often chefs bring out special flavors in their meats by the use of such world-famous sauces as béarnaise (white wine, shallots, butter and egg yolks) or bourguignonne (red wine, herbs, mushroom skins and butter). Opposite is a list of the names of basic French meat dishes with a rough translation of what they are. Note: Most steaks come to the table with the bone cut out. The French prefer their lamb rarer than Americans generally do, and it is well to order it *bien cuit*, or well done. For a rare steak, say that you want it *bleu* or *saignant*. Medium rare is *à point*.

Fish, Fowl and Vegetables All through the night, fast trains and trucks bring to Paris fresh fish from the coasts, fowl and vegetables from the farms. The list below translates names of the more frequently served foods.

Boeuf—Beef
BIFTECK A thick slice of fillet or sirloin

BOEUF BOURGUIGNON A beef stew cooked with red wine

CHÂTEAUBRIAND Porterhouse steak

ENTRECÔTE Medium-sized rib steak, usually grilled or fried

FAUX-FILET OR CONTRE-FILET A sirloin steak

FILET DE BOEUF Tenderloin

FILET MIGNON The center of the fillet

POT-AU-FEU Beef and vegetable stew

Veau—Veal
BLANQUETTE DE VEAU Veal stew

CERVELLE DE VEAU Calf's brains

CÔTES DE VEAU Veal chops

ESCALOPE DE VEAU A thin slice cut from the fillet or rib

FOIE DE VEAU Calf's liver

NOIX DE VEAU Pieces of roasted veal cut from the rump

RIS DE VEAU Sweetbreads

ROGNONS DE VEAU Veal kidneys

Agneau—Lamb
CARRÉ D'AGNEAU Rib roast

CÔTELETTES D'AGNEAU Lamb chops

GIGOT Leg of lamb

POITRINE D'AGNEAU Breast of lamb

Porc—Pork
CARRÉ DE PORC Loin of pork

CHARCUTERIE Specialty meats of all kinds, particularly pork products but may include beef or veal

COCHON DE LAIT Suckling pig

CÔTELETTES DE PORC Pork chops

JAMBON Ham

Poisson—Fish
ÉCREVISSE Crayfish

HOMARD Lobster

HUÎTRES Oysters (many varieties; the best are *Belon* and *Marennes*; others may be too salty for your taste)

MOULES Mussels

SAUMON Salmon

THON Tuna fish

TRUITE Trout

Volaille—Fowl
CANARD Duck

CANETON Duckling

DINDE, DINDONNEAU Turkey

FAISAN Pheasant

PINTADE Guinea hen

POULET Chicken

Other Meats
GRENOUILLE Frog

LAPIN Rabbit

Légumes—Vegetables
CHAMPIGNONS Mushrooms

CHOU Cabbage

CHOU-FLEUR Cauliflower

CRESSON Water cress

ÉPINARDS Spinach

FLAGEOLETS Baby lima beans

HARICOTS VERTS String beans

LAITUE Lettuce

OIGNON Onion

PETITS POIS Peas

POMMES DE TERRE Potatoes

RIZ Rice

Cheeses   The French eat cheese as part of every meal except breakfast. They always eat it before the dessert, usually washing it down with what is left of their wine. As the great gastronome Brillat-Savarin remarked, "a dessert without cheese is like a pretty girl with only one eye." All restaurants offer cheeses on every menu, and it is a mistake to pass up this traditional part of a classic French meal. The great French cheeses are known the world round—Camembert, Brie, Roquefort, Port-Salut. In addition you might try Pont-l'Evêque, a softish, fermented type, Fromage de Chèvre, or goat's cheese, or any of the excellent French cream cheeses. The French eat their Camembert and Brie less well matured than do Americans and it is wise to order them *bien fait,* or well done.

Wines   The wines of France, Frenchmen agree, are the best in the world and, enthusiastically, the world concurs. But selecting one to go with the *châteaubriand* you have just chosen for your dinner is complicated. Should the wine be red, white or *rosé?* Should it come from the golden slopes of Burgundy or one of the tiny vineyards that tip up to face the southern sun in the valley of the Rhône or from the hot plains of Bordeaux or from Beaujolais? And when you have finally settled on the region of France and even the very vineyard the wine must come from, then which is the best year for that wine that you can afford? The solution is to call over the *sommelier,* or wine steward (you can tell him because he usually carries the symbolic keys of the cellar), and place yourself in his hands. This man, merely by drawing the right cork, has the power to transport you to heaven.

Of course, selecting wines for a more modest meal does not have to be that complicated. A good Beaujolais (red wine) is fine with anything that is not fish. *Rosé,* a pink wine, is also good with any food except game. Just remember the basic rules: red wines go with any meat course; white wines are for the fish. Then consult the listing below that shows the best recent years for all the major wine-making areas; asterisks indicate exceptionally good years. With this and a wine card you will be able to work out a happy selection. And finally, if the whole thing seems too complicated, just stare at the waiter and order a glass of Château la Pompe (tap water). He'll grin back at you and ask which year you would prefer.

RED BORDEAUX	*1945	*1947	1948	1949	1950	1952
	*1953	*1955	1957	1958	1959	
WHITE BORDEAUX	*1945	*1947	1948	1949	1952	*1953
	*1955	*1957	1959			
RED BURGUNDIES	*1945	*1947	1948	1949	1952	*1953
	*1955	1957	*1959			
WHITE BURGUNDIES	1945	1946	*1947	1948	*1949	1952
	1955	1957	*1959			
BEAUJOLAIS—MÂCONNAIS	*1945	1946	1947	1948	1949	1952
	*1953	1955	1957	*1959		
CÔTES DU RHÔNE	*1945	1946	*1947	1948	1949	1950
	1952	1955	1956	1957		
LOIRE	*1945	1946	*1947	1949	1950	1952
	*1953	1955	1957	1958	*1959	
ALSACE	*1945	1946	*1947	1948	1949	1950
	1952	1953	1954	1955	1957	*1959
CHAMPAGNE	1945	1946	*1947	1949	1952	1953
	1955	1957	*1959			

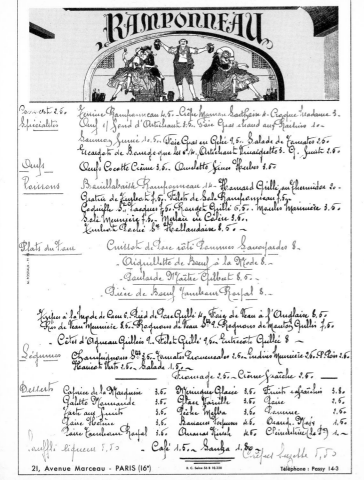

Deciphering a French menu The menu reproduced on this page is a fair sample of the rather bewildering documents used in any of the better restaurants. Even full size—the original of this one measures a foot by a foot and a half—they are hard to read, for they are frequently written in crowded and ornate French script and the choice of dishes offered is confusingly wide. The notes below, keyed to the menu's main divisions (*far left*), will guide the diner.

COUVERT This word, in the upper left-hand corner, means the setting, that is, the silver, napkin, water and bread (not butter). In effect, it is a cover charge of 50 cents.

SPÉCIALITÉS In the case of the Ramponneau this means the *hors-d'oeuvre* in which the chef takes a particular pride. These are reproduced here in blue; usually they appear in red on the menu. Below these special *hors-d'oeuvre* appear others.

OEUFS If the diner is very hungry he can have eggs in cream sauce or an omelet as a starter.

POISSONS Only one specialty, reproduced here in blue, is listed: it is a *bouillabaisse,* a rich fish stew.

PLATS DU JOUR These are the main dishes of the day. This menu of the Ramponneau offers two beef dishes, roast pork and chicken. Below these are dishes from pigs' feet to a steak.

LÉGUMES Vegetables are separately ordered in French restaurants, cost extra and are eaten after the main dish. The French normally order a salad. A starchy vegetable usually comes with the main course.

FROMAGE Cheese forms an essential part of a French meal. The diner need only choose his favorite from a tray.

DESSERTS Although desserts are in blue ink here, they are *not* the house specialties in this restaurant. Here the specials are at the bottom, *Soufflé liqueur* and *Crêpes Suzette*. Fruits and pastries are also offered.

CAFÉ Coffee is served at the end of the meal, never with a main course.

THE WONDERFUL
RESTAURANTS OF PARIS

Because French mothers make sure to instill high culinary standards in their young at the family table, French chefs must be good. They know that nothing can equal the cold fury of a Frenchman whose chef has let him down. The dish is insultingly rejected; the client fumes. Keeping chefs to mark, true Parisians believe, is the reason superb restaurants abound in all corners of their city.

The list on the pages that follow is a fair sampling of the best and the most interesting restaurants in several price categories. Some are famous and expensive, others are quiet little places that are not so expensive, and a few are neighborhood *bistros* that have turned up a first-rate chef. They are grouped alphabetically according to sections of the city. To find a particular restaurant you may know, refer to the Index (*page 199*). In each listing there are daggers. One dagger means that a three-course average meal without wine will cost under 20 NF; two daggers means the cost will be from 20 to 30 NF, and three daggers means over 30 NF, but this last figure *can* go as high as 75 NF. The price of wine can vary from 5 NF to 50 NF.

Champs-Élysées—Ternes

LE BERKELEY
7 Avenue Matignon (58, M-4) BAL 47-79. Open every day
††† Luxurious, serene atmosphere and good food. Popular with stage and movie people.

LE BERRI
2 Rue de Berri (58, H-3) ELY 12-65. Open every day
† Convenient to the Champs-Élysées, Le Berri offers a good layout of *hors-d'oeuvre*, half a dozen simple main dishes and excellent éclairs. It also can fashion, on request, a fine plate of bacon and eggs. A good, small, convenient restaurant.

LE CABARET
4 Avenue Franklin D. Roosevelt (58, L-6) ELY 20-98. Closed Saturdays July through October
†† A smartly decorated restaurant with good sea food.
• *Specialties: Filet de sole Cabaret, Côte de boeuf grillée.*

CRILLON GRILL ROOM
Hôtel de Crillon, 10 Place de la Concorde (58, Q-5) ANJ 24-10. Open every day
††† An agreeable modern room in a famous hotel where the food is good and well served.

• *Specialties: Oeufs à la bénédictine, Steak châteaubriand.*

L'ÉTOILE (POTEL)
4 Avenue Victor-Hugo (58, D-2) PAS 69-46. Closed Mondays and August
†† The restaurant Potel on the second floor deserves its fame.
• *Specialties: Sole farcie Victor Hugo, Tournedos des gourmets, Feuilleté Napoléon.*

FOUQUET'S
99 Avenue des Champs-Élysées (58, G-3) BAL 59-54. Open every day
†† Once one of the fabled names in Parisian dining, its main attraction now is the vast spread of tables out on the sidewalk. But people who come are interesting, the food is still good and dinner can be had as late as 2 a.m.

CHEZ FRANCIS
7 Place de l'Alma (58, G-7) ELY 79-11. Open every day
†† A smart spot where businessmen meet each other and, in the evenings, their wives. The food is solid and simple, and the bartender knows how to make a good martini.
• *Specialty: Châteaubriand grillé.*

CHEZ GEORGES
273 Bd Péreire (126, A-1) ETO 31-00.

Closed Saturdays and July 15-August 20

† Out of the way, but perhaps worth it to have good French food in surroundings with a slightly rustic and provincial air.

• *Specialties: Gigot, Éclairs.*

GEORGE-V

31 Avenue George-V (58, G-4) BAL 35-30. Open every day

††† Perhaps the best hotel-restaurant in Paris. It offers diners a wide choice of dishes.

JOSEPH

56 Rue Pierre-Charron (58, H-4) ELY 63-25. Closed Sundays

†† A quiet restaurant where the service is discreet and the food classic. The clientele is elegant, often famous.

• *Specialties: Omelette maison, Poulet Joseph, Steak châteaubriand.*

LASSERRE

17 Avenue Franklin D. Roosevelt (58, L-6) ELY 53-43. Closed Sundays

††† One of the best in the world, according to many gourmets. The menu is elaborate, the wines fine, the service excellent, the prices high. Particularly delightful in summer when the roof of the upstairs dining room is opened to the stars.

• *Specialties: Feuilleté de langoustines*

Kermer, Steak Dumas, Casserolette de filets de sole Lasserre, Poularde Grand Palais, Pannequet soufflé flambé.

LAURENT

41 Avenue Gabriel (58, M-4) ELY 14-49. Closed Sundays and August 15-31

††† A handsome place overlooking the gardens of the Champs-Élysées. Dining outside in the summer. The food is superior, the service good, prices high.

• *Specialties: Soufflé de homard, Escalope de veau Angelo, Rognons au Chambertin.*

LEDOYEN

Jardin des Champs-Élysées (58, M-4) ANJ 47-82. Closed August

††† In the gardens of the Champs-Élysées. Summer dining on a terrace surrounded by grass and flowers. The setting is superior to the cuisine.

• *Specialties: Sole Ledoyen, Côte de boeuf grillée, Tarte Tatin.*

MARIUS ET JANETTE

4 Avenue George-V (58, G-6) ELY 71-78. Closed August

†† A very good provincial restaurant with a terrace for summer dining.

• *Specialties: Fish and shellfish.*

PLAZA ATHÉNÉE

25 Avenue Montaigne (58, J-6) BAL 14-90. Open every day

††† The restaurant is as agreeable as

the hotel. Excellent food. Right in the center of the fashion world, this has been a meeting place of the rich and fashionable for generations. The "Relais," a smaller restaurant, is expensive but great for snacks.

• *Specialties: Soufflé de homard, Tournedos Plaza, Pêche royale.*

PRUNIER TRAKTIR

16 Avenue Victor-Hugo (58, C-2) PAS 01-45. Closed Mondays and August

†† For over 60 years a fashionable sea food restaurant. The oysters are excellent. Dinner is served until 10 p.m.

• *Specialties: Brochette St-Jacques, Marmite dieppoise.*

RAMPONNEAU

21 Avenue Marceau (58, F-6) PAS 14-31. Closed Mondays

†† A tastefully decorated and generally excellent restaurant that serves many of the classic French dishes and has a superior wine cellar.

• *Specialties: Turbot soufflé, Pâble de lièvre flambé.*

LE ROND-POINT

1 Avenue Matignon (58, L-4) ELY 38-70. Open every day

†† Handily located at the Rond-Point des Champs-Élysées. The cooking is good, in the semi-Spanish style of the Basque country.

• *Specialties: Oeufs poêlés Ramuntcho, Paëlla biscaïenne.*

SAINT-JEAN-PIED-DE-PORT

123 Av. de Wagram (Paris map, front end paper, E-2) CAR 61-50. Open every day

†† Very good Basque restaurant not far from the Étoile, with an emphasis on southern French fish dishes.

CHEZ TANTE LOUISE

41 Rue Boissy-d'Anglas (58, Q-3) ANJ 28-19. Closed Sundays and August

†† Small and intimate. The food is good, the service stylish and careful.

• *Specialties: Quenelles de brochet Nantua. Coq au vin jurassienne.*

AUBERGE DE LA TRUITE

30 Rue de Faubourg-St-Honoré (58, Q-4) ANJ 12-86. Closed Sundays and August

†† An intimate restaurant and bar in a courtyard just off the smartest shopping street in Paris. Genuine 18th Century Norman rustic style, with visible beams and carved woodwork. As the name implies, the specialties are fish.

RELAIS DE VENISE-ENTRECÔTE

271 Boulevard Péreire (126, A-1) ETO 58-77. Closed Fridays and July

† The only main course at this *bistro* is steak. A dessert to remember is *Vacherin du relais* (vanilla ice cream balls floating in hot chocolate sauce).

Number and letter combinations in parentheses are map references; i.e., "(127, T-5)" means page 127, location T-5.

Opéra-Grands Boulevards

CAFÉ DE LA PAIX

12 Boulevard des Capucines (127, T-6) OPE 35-44. Open every day
†† The café section is world renowned. There is no better place to sit at a sidewalk table, enjoy delicious ice creams, drink excellent coffee and watch Parisians stroll by. The ornate restaurant, once a favorite before or after the Opéra, is not as fine as formerly, but the food and the wine cellar are still very good.

DROUANT

18 Rue Gaillon (127, U-7) OPE 53-72. Closed August
††† A widely known sea food restaurant of superior quality. Founded in 1880, it has been for decades the meeting place of the Académie Goncourt, a most influential literary society. The *décor* is comfortably old-fashioned.
• *Specialties: Sole au champagne, Coquille de homard Drouant, Quenelles de brochet.*

LABORDERIE

17 Rue Bergère (127, Z-5) PRO 95-87. Closed Sundays and August
†† Excellent Basque cooking at a reasonable price.
• *Specialties: Rosette de langue Toulouse, Omelette de la maison, Galantine de dinde armagnac.*

LAVERGNE

51 Rue du Faubourg-St-Martin (138, P-10) NOR 58-42. Closed Sundays and July 10-August 31
†† Appropriately decorated to go with the rich *bouillabaisse* and other Mediterranean sea food dishes.
• *Specialties: Palourdes farcies et grillées, Rognons de veau Lavergne.*

LUCAS-CARTON

9 Place de la Madeleine (126, R-6) ANJ 22-90. Open every day
††† A pleasant, quiet spot to eat lunch after a tiring morning of sight-seeing or shopping on the Faubourg-St-Honoré. Classic Parisian cuisine. Very French.

CHEZ MAX À L'ARCADE

19 Rue de Castellane (126, R-5) ANJ 33-81. Closed Sundays, holidays and August
†† An excellent *bistro* with a flair for delicious food. Simple *décor*.
• *Specialties: Foie gras frais, Agneau de lait.*

MAXIM'S

3 Rue Royale (126, Q-8) ANJ 27-94. Closed Sundays
††† The luxurious dining room, scene of legendary naughtiness at the turn of the century, is so celebrated that a visitor might still want to eat here despite the very high prices and the rather short shrift waiters and chefs tend to give tourists.

MEURICE

228 Rue de Rivoli (127, S-9) OPE 32-40. Open every day
††† Its kitchen has catered to royalty for over a century. Sumptuous *décor* with gilded woodwork, marble, paintings and glittering chandeliers.

PRUNIER

9 Rue Duphot (126, R-7) OPE 11-40. Closed Mondays and June 30-August 31
††† Divided into a dozen rooms of various sizes, Prunier's is a fine old sea food restaurant and the best place to stop off for a dozen oysters.
• *Specialties: Langoustine sauce champagne, Filet de turbot Verilhac.*

LA QUETSCH

6 Rue des Capucines (127, S-7) OPE 90-09. Closed Sundays, principal holidays and three weeks in August
†† A delicatessen counter on the ground floor serves quick fancy snacks. The restaurant upstairs has French and foreign foods and efficient service. One of the few places in the center of Paris for after-theater dining.
• *Specialties: 164 hors-d'oeuvre from 24 nations. Poulet mâconnais à la crème, Tarte maison, Crêpes Rothschild.*

RITZ

15 Place Vendôme (127, S-8) OPE 28-30. Open every day
††† The Ritz Hotel has two excellent restaurants—the turn of the century-styled dining room, with faded pastel-painted ceilings, mirrors, statues and plants, and green and beige woodwork; and the Espadon, a modern grill. The latter is noted for its sea food, and both are, of course, famous as elegant meeting places of the famous.

RÔTISSERIE REINE PÉDAUQUE

6 Rue de la Pépinière (126, Q-3) LAB 86-90. Open every day
†† Several small rooms with beamed ceilings and colored windowpanes give a quiet, contented, country inn atmosphere under the coat of arms of Burgundy. The food is solid, with Burgundian specialties. Good Burgundy wine is put on each table in magnum bottles; you pay only for what you drink.

TABLE DU ROY

10 Cité d'Antin (127, U-4) TRI 08-43. Closed Sundays and August
††† Small and jolly. The chef, posing as a king, selects your dinner and you have little to say about it. But the food is solidly French and well cooked.
• *Specialties: Caneton au madère, Langouste au coulis d'écrevisses, Crêpes Suzette.*

† Symbols indicate average cost of a three-course meal without wine: † under 20 NF; †† 20-30 NF; ††† from 30 NF on up.

Palais-Royal—Marais

CHEZ L'AMI LOUIS
*32 Rue Vertbois (104, M-1) TUR 77-48.
Closed Tuesdays and August*
††† A charming and excellent Basque restaurant. Game of all kinds in their seasons are the house specialties.

LA BOULE D'OR
*15 Place d'Aligre (105, S-10) DID 93-70.
Closed Fridays and July 15-September 1*
††† One of the three *bistro*-style restaurants that are recognized as having extremely fine food. Located in an ancient and interesting building near the Bastille. Reservation necessary.
• *Specialties: Quiche lorraine, Côte de veau paprika, Filets de sole au vermouth.*

CAVEAU MONTPENSIER
15 Rue de Montpensier (104, B-1) RIC 82-96. Open every day
† A candlelit 17th Century cellar decorated with ancient armor and modern paintings. Especially good for a midnight snack after the Comédie Française next door. Music every evening and a show during the winter.
• *Specialty: Escargots.*

COCHON D'OR
*31 Rue du Jour (104, F-2) CEN 38-31.
Open from 4 a.m. to 2 p.m. Closed Sundays and August*

† This excellent *bistro*, which caters to the early-rising men of Les Halles, is the perfect place to finish a long night.

COCONNAS
2 bis Place des Vosges (104, O-7) ARC 58-16. Closed Tuesdays
††† The food is very good, the *décor* rich, the view of Place des Vosges picturesque.
• *Specialties: Poule du bon Roy Henry, Merlan "Coconnas," Tarte des demoiselles Tatin.*

GRAND VÉFOUR
17 Rue de Beaujolais (104, B-1) RIC 58-97. Closed Sundays and August
††† A great restaurant since the time of Napoleon, it is one of the very best in the world today, but expensive. The food, wine and service are perfect and the furnishings have an 18th Century charm.
• *Specialties: Lamproie bordelaise, Ortolans, Bécasse bordelaise.*

LAVIGNE
30 Rue de l'Arbre-Sec (104, D-4) CEN 62-60. Closed Tuesdays and August
† A comfortable, family-run *bistro* with simple *décor* and a large bowl of flowers. Its capacity is 30 people.
• *Specialties: Steak and sea food.*

CHEZ PAULINE
*5 Rue Villedo (104, B-1) RIC 45-98.
Closed Sundays and August*
† Quality cooking in the style of Lyon, long the capital of French gastronomy.
• *Specialties: Entrecôte à la moelle, Mousse au chocolat.*

PHARAMOND
24 Rue de la Grande Truanderie (104, G-2) GUT 06-72. Closed Sundays
†† Located in the middle of town, the Pharamond provides the standard Parisian cuisine prepared to perfection.
• *Specialties: Coquilles St-Jacques, Tripes à la mode de Caen, Steak grillé Châteaubriand, Pommes soufflées.*

AUX DUCS DE BOURGOGNE
*2 Place d'Anvers (138, J-5) TRU 35-21.
Closed Sundays*
†† Good, rich Burgundy cooking.
• *Specialties: Escargots, Rognons de veau.*

AUBERGE DU PÈRE LOUIS
7 Rue de la Boule-Rouge (138, J-10) PRO 95-49. Open every day
† Pleasant and modest, with food of the classic French type. Near the Folies-Bergère.
• *Specialty: Poulet à la broche.*

KUNTZ
31 Rue d'Alsace 10E (138, P-7) NOR 53-54. Open every day
† First-rate Alsatian food; generally a fine restaurant.
• *Specialties: Escargots à l'alsacienne,*

AU ROY GOURMET
4 Place des Victoires (104, D-1) LOU 10-16. Closed Saturday nights, Sundays and August
†† Good family-style food, friendly atmosphere, comfortable leather benches.
• *Specialties: Filets de sole maison, Steak "Roy Gourmet."*

Montmartre—Pigalle

Truite en gelée au Riesling, Potée aux haricots rouges.

LE RELAIS DE LA BUTTE
*12 Rue Ravignan (138, G-3) MON 16-18.
Closed Thursdays and August*
†† A tiny old Montmartre inn with gay, bright curtains, candlelight and the finest food on the Butte. The sign over the door reads, "You feel so good in Montmartre that you want to leave only to go to heaven."
• *Specialties: Soupe à l'oignon, Poulet à l'armagnac, Grenouilles, Escargots.*

A LA MÈRE CATHERINE
*6 Place du Tertre (138, H-2) MON 32-69.
Open every day*
††† A fine old restaurant with food that will please a healthy appetite.

Number and letter combinations in parentheses are map references; i.e., "(127, T-5)" means page 127, location T-5.

NICOLAS

12 Rue de la Fidélité (138, O-10) PRO 10-72. Closed August

† Moderately priced, near the Gare de l'Est, with sawdust on the floor and good wine in carafes.

• *Specialties: Feuilleté de fruits de mer, Steak au poivre.*

Islands—Latin Quarter

CHEZ ALLARD

41 Rue St-André des Arts (26, N-3) DAN 48-23. Closed Sundays and July 15-September 1

†† The very best of the *bistros*. The food is excellent and the portions staggeringly generous. Two small dining rooms in a handsome Louis XIII house seat only 40; reservations should be made 48 hours in advance.

• *Specialties: Entrecôte marchand de vin, Veau à la berrichonne,* and *Turbot beurre blanc.*

RELAIS BISSON

37 Quai des Grands-Augustins (26, O-2) DAN 71-80. Closed Sundays and August

††† An excellent, fashionable restaurant with a view of the Seine. The sea food dishes are especially good.

CALVET

165 Boulevard St-Germain (26, K-3) LIT 93-51. Closed Sundays and August

††† A terrace makes this an attractive

place to have "classic" food on a warm summer evening. Reservations are advisable because the terrace is small.

• *Specialties: Canard à l'orange, Coq en pâte.*

CHEZ CHATAIGNER

75 Rue du Cherche-Midi (26, F-6) LIT 82-74. Closed Sundays and Mondays, and July and August

††† A homey little restaurant in an unfrequented quarter of the Left Bank. The food is superb, especially the fish and lobster, and the wines are excellent.

LA CHOPE DANTON

4 Carrefour de l'Odéon (26, M-4) DAN 67-76. Closed Mondays and August

†† A place for simple, satisfying food. Waiters lavish their attention on regular customers, but the tourist is not wholly neglected and the restaurant is handy to the Théâtre de France and the lively Odéon neighborhood.

• *Specialties: Steak au poivre, Jambon*

à la crème, Grenouilles à la provençale, Coquilles St-Jacques, Côte de veau à la crème.

COCHON DE LAIT

7 Rue Corneille (26, N-5) DAN 03-65. Open every day

†† A large, red-tablecloth restaurant near the Théâtre de France that specializes in pork dishes, grilled steaks and chops. Reasonable and good. You can watch meats being roasted in the open grill.

LAPÉROUSE

51 Quai des Grands-Augustins (26, N-1) DAN 68-04. Closed Sundays during June, July and August

††† One of the very great and very expensive restaurants; overlooking the Seine; several small, comfortable and elegant dining rooms. The panels in one of the small *salons* are said to have been painted by Boucher.

• *Specialties: Gratin de langoustines Georgette, Poulet docteur.*

CHEZ MARIUS

30 Rue des Fossés-St-Bernard (27, S-6) ODE 19-01. Closed Sundays and August

†† An ideal place to have lunch or dinner after a walk around the Île St-Louis or a trip to the nearby Halles-aux-Vins.

• *Specialties: Homard à l'Américaine,*

Bouillabaisse (Fridays), *Coq au vin.*

MÉDITERRANÉE

2 Place de l'Odéon (26, M-5) ODE 44-30. Open every day

††† One of the best-known sea food restaurants, recently redecorated, with a sunny terrace. The cooking is provincial and good.

• *Specialties: Bouillabaisse, Bourride.*

RÔTISSERIE PÉRIGOURDINE

2 Place St-Michel (26, P-3) DAN 70-54. Closed Fridays

††† A pleasant, airy place to have lunch on a hot day, with big windows looking out over the bookstalls and the Seine. Truffles in all their forms and uses are the specialty of the house.

AU PETIT CHÂTELET

39 Rue de la Bûcherie (26, Q-4) ODE 17-95. Closed Sundays and August 15-September 15

†† A charming little restaurant with excellent service and food. Built above the foundation of Paris' ancient Châtelet fortress.

RELAIS DE PORQUEROLLES

12 Rue de l'Éperon (26, N-3) ODE 44-30. Closed Sundays and July and August

††† An exceedingly attractive restaurant with fine sea food cooked in the fashion of southern France.

RELAIS PARIS-EST

In the Cour d'Honneur de la Gare de l'Est (138, P-8) NOR 81-63. Closed Sundays

††† Probably the finest railroad station restaurant in the world. Worth a visit for the food, plain but efficient service.

• *Specialties: Délices de sole, Mignonnette d'agneau Charmereine.*

† *Symbols indicate average cost of a three-course meal with wine:* † *under 20 NF;* †† *20-30 NF;* ††† *from 30 NF on up.*

- *Specialties: Bouillabaisse, Pipérade, Paëlla, Confit d'oie.*

LA TOUR D'ARGENT

15 Quai de la Tournelle (27, S-5) ODE 22-31. Closed Mondays

††† Not as good as it once was but just as expensive, the Tour d'Argent is still one of the world's greatest restaurants. Elegant in its red and white *décor*, it overlooks the Seine, Notre-Dame and the Right Bank. The view is breathtaking on nights when the floodlights illuminate Paris' great public buildings.

Montparnasse-Invalides

CLOSERIE DES LILAS

171 Boulevard du Montparnasse (26, L-10) DAN 70-50. Open every day

††† A delightful place to dine outside on a warm summer evening, between the Observatoire and the Luxembourg Gardens. The broad terrace, framed in hedges and sheltered by chestnut trees, has been a favorite of writers and artists—Baudelaire, Ingres, Picasso, Braque—for a century, and the food, service and wine are very good. Empire *décor* and an American bar.

LES MARRONNIERS

53 bis Boulevard Arago (Paris map, front end paper J-9) POR 58-57. Closed Wednesdays; also August 15-31 and February 15-28

†† A small room and a small terrace

- *Specialties: Croustade de barbue Lagrené, Caneton Tour d'Argent.*

AUBERGE DU VERT-GALANT

42 Quai des Orfèvres (26, O-1) DAN 83-68. Open every day till midnight

††† Old and luxurious, with fine food and excellent service. Dining on a terrace by the side of the Seine. It bears the nickname of France's King Henri IV, who loved fine food and beautiful women.

- *Specialties: Soufflé de barbue, Poule au pot, Pannequets.*

seat between them only 20, so make a reservation. The menu is written on a slate. In short, an intimate and informal place. The food is excellent, the wines very good.

- *Specialties: Sole St-André au whisky, Suprême de volaille aux morilles, Langouste à l'américaine, Coquilles St-Jacques maison.*

LA BOURGOGNE

6 Avenue Bosquet (88, N-3) SOL 96-78. Closed Sundays and August

†† Excellent Burgundy cooking, which is to say both high in calories and highly delicious. Smart, simple, quiet.

- *Specialties: Oeufs en meurette, Fricassée de petits gris aux croutons, Steak bourguignon à la moelle.*

TOUR EIFFEL

Champ-de-Mars (88, K-5) INV 88-80. The first-floor restaurant: open every day; closed January 1-February 28. Second-floor restaurant: open every day for lunch

† There is, of course, an extraordinary view of Paris from either the restaurant on the first floor of the Eiffel Tower or from the grill room on the second floor. The food in the first-floor restaurant is much better than that in the grill room.

CHEZ FRANÇOISE

Aérogare des Invalides (88, R-2) INV 87-00. Open every day

† A good restaurant in the downtown air terminal.

L'ORÉE DU BOIS

Pte Maillot (151, U-10) MAI 78-04. Open every day

†† Large and modern, it has two big terraces giving on the Bois de Boulogne. At dinner there is dancing and a show.

- *Specialties: Sole à la crème maison*

PAVILLON ROYAL

Face au Grand Lac; Bois de Boulogne (150 P-8) PAS 92-00. Open March-November

††† A fine restaurant in a grand mansion, incomparably situated on the shore of the large lake in the Bois de Boulogne.

- *Specialties: Jambon madère, Truffles St-Hubert.*

CHEZ LUCIEN

12 Rue Surcouf (88, Q-3) INV 46-93. Closed Thursdays

†† Small and rustic, with good food.

MONT-BLANC

2 Rue Casimir-Périer (89, T-4) INV 58-40. Closed Sundays

†† Good provincial cuisine, served in generous portions. *Décor* is plain, clientele mostly solid French citizens.

- *Specialties: Bouillabaisse; Rognons de veau à la fine Champagne; Steak flambé Mont-Blanc.*

Bois de Boulogne

LE PETIT BEDON

38 Rue Pergolèse (58, A-1) PAS 23-66. Closed Mondays and August 15 through September 10

††† A small, smart restaurant with excellent food and a wide choice of dishes.

- *Specialties: Omelette aux queues d'crevices Curnousky, Truffes sous la cendre, Noisette d'agneau à l'estragon.*

PRÉ CATELAN

Bois de Boulogne (150, M-6) AUT 05-60. Open from March to November

††† The charm here is the setting in the woods; you can dine and dance outside by lantern. Expensive.

Number and letter combinations in parentheses are map references; i.e., "(127, T-5)" means page 127, location T-5.

Non-French Restaurants Paris, acknowledged leader in fine eating, is sufficiently cosmopolitan to justify the existence of a number of dining places catering to the tastes of the many nationality groups living in this city. Although the city does not offer the wide variety of foreign restaurants existing elsewhere, there are some good ones.

AUBERGE DE LA CLOCHE

30 Rue St-André-des-Arts (26, O-3) ODE 92-22. Closed Tuesdays and August
†† A Russian restaurant frequented by Paris' Russian colony. Authentic food and 30 kinds of *hors-d'oeuvre*. Sturdy tables and tavernlike paneling.

CHEZ BEULEMANS

204 Boulevard St-Germain (26, H-2) LIT 73-30. Closed Tuesdays
† Good Belgian food, cozy setting.
• *Specialties: Ragoût de poulet, Poulet à la crème, Asperges Béarnaise.*

CHEZ LOUIS

14 Rue Lincoln (58, H-3) ELY 36-14. Closed Saturday nights, Sundays and August
†† Not very handsome, but open late and the Viennese food is of superior quality.

COPENHAGUE

142 Avenue des Champs-Élysées (58, F-2) ELY 20-41. Open every day
†† The smorgasbord of Danish delica-cies is lavish although the *décor* lacks charm. The comfortable bar is a good place to meet for drinks.

FLOTOUR

9 Boulevard du Montparnasse (26, D-7) SEG 68-15. Open every day
† The most colorful Chinese restaurant in Paris. The waiters dress in flowing robes and the ceiling is covered with golden dragons. There are 108 dishes, of which the most unusual is shark's lips served on crisp pancakes.

GOLDENBERG

7 Rue des Rosiers (104, M-6) TUR 20-16. Closed Saturdays and on Jewish holidays
† A fine Jewish restaurant with a delicatessen counter that contains everyone's favorite spicy meats and pickles. A good spot to pick up sandwiches before a drive or a walk.

MAISONNETTE RUSSE

6 Rue d'Armaillé (126, C-2) ETO 56-04. Closed Mondays and August
†† A Russian restaurant, once known as Auberge d'Armaillé, with a vast assortment of *hors-d'oeuvre* and fine main dishes. All three *prix fixe* menus include all the vodka you can drink.
• *Specialties: Côtelette Kieff, Timbale Catherine la Grande.*

PAPRIKA

14 Rue Chauchat (127, W-4) PRO 19-01
† Classic Hungarian dishes and music

SAN FRANCISCO

1 Rue Mirabeau (88, A-10) MIR 75-44. Closed Mondays and July and August
††† A fine Italian restaurant on the outskirts of Auteuil.
• *Specialties: Saltimbocca alla Romana, Tagliarini with sea food.*

Cafés Almost every street corner in Paris is graced by a café. In good weather, of course, the Parisians' favorite time-spending device is sitting at a sidewalk table in front of a café watching other Parisians stroll by. Most cafés serve only the traditional French *apéritifs*, coffee, wine and beer. Some serve sandwiches and ice cream. Cocktails and whisky are usually not available. (See Cocktail Bars, page 175.) The list below gives the names of cafés of particular interest.

BRASSERIE LIPP

151 Boulevard St-Germain (26, K-3). Closed on holidays
A good place for a hefty sandwich and glass of beer late at night. One of the centers of Paris night life.

CAFÉ DES DEUX MAGOTS

170 Boulevard St-Germain (26, K-2). Open every day
Famous after World War II as a gathering place of existentialist writers, this is still a good, comfortable café with a spread of sidewalk tables. The two *magots* are wooden figures of oriental wise men. Open until 2 a.m.

CAFÉ DE FLORE

172 Boulevard St-Germain (26, K-2). Open every day
Several comfortable rooms and a small spread of sidewalk tables (enclosed and warmed in winter) still have an intellectual aura although the existentialists have moved on and young American students have moved in.

† Symbols indicate average cost of a three-course meal without wine: † under 20 NF; †† 20-30 NF; ††† from 30 NF on up.

CAFÉ DE LA RÉGENCE

161 Rue St-Honoré (59, U-7). Open every day 9 a.m.-2 a.m.
Probably the oldest café still existing in Paris, the Régence was once patronized by Rousseau and Voltaire. Napoleon was but one of the many chess players who have gathered here.

CAFÉ DE LA PAIX

12 Boulevard des Capucines (127, T-6). Open every day
A large and comfortable sidewalk terrace has always been the chief attraction of this famous café. Near American Express, most banks and the main shopping district; it is a perfect place to take a short rest and watch everybody else hurry by. The eating places inside—a grill, a snack room and a restaurant—are all good.

LA COUPOLE

102 Boulevard du Montparnasse (26, H-9). Closed August 1-21

Sandwiches and Quick Snacks
There are several snack bars and hamburger stands in Paris which cater primarily to American tourists homesick for familiar dishes, though many Frenchmen can be found at them too. A partial listing follows.

LE DRUGSTORE

133 Avenue des Champs-Élysées (58, F-2). Open every day

A snack bar, with Wild West *décor*, serves sandwiches, hot dishes and the most authentic ice cream sundaes on

Popular in the 1920s, this café is coming back into fashion as a meeting place for artists and intellectuals. Open until 3 a.m. Saturday nights, 2 a.m. other nights.

LE DÔME

108 Boulevard du Montparnasse (26, H-9). Open every day
Students and artists still jam this famous spot. Open until 2 a.m. upstairs, all night downstairs.

FOUQUET'S

99 Avenue des Champs-Élysées (58, G-3). Open every day
A view of the entire Champs-Élysées can be had from the terrace. An opulent restaurant and bar are inside.

LE SELECT

99 Boulevard du Montparnasse (26, H-9). Open every day
An inevitable stop for Lady Brett and her coterie during *The Sun Also Rises* era.

the Continent. There is a pharmacy, newsstand and a gift counter. Patronized by starlets, models and, of course, tourists. Almost always crowded.

PAM-PAM

5 Place de l'Opéra (127, T-6). Open every day until 1 a.m.
Sandwiches, ice cream, bacon and eggs for the homesick tourist. Close to the American Express, Opéra and shopping district, but crowded.

WIMPY'S HAMBURGERS

9 Boulevard des Italiens (127, W-5). Open 6:30 a.m. to 2 a.m.

8 Boulevard de Clichy (138, G-5). Open 10 a.m. to 2 a.m.

2 Rue du 4-Septembre (127, W-7). Open 7:30 a.m. to 11:30 p.m. Closed Sundays
The hamburgers are small but good and not expensive. Sandwiches, coffee, tea, wine and beer. Take-out orders are neatly packaged in Cellophane at no extra charge.

Self-Service
In addition to American-style snack bars there are more than 40 self-service cafeterias in Paris (often distinguished by the words *libre service* in addition to a name). Most of them offer a filling French meal for about 4 NF. A partial list follows.

LIBRE SERVICE

34 Av. des Champs-Élysées (58, K-4). Open every day

LES ESSAIS

40 Av. Montaigne (58, J-6). Open every day

LE GRAND VATEL

275 R. St-Honoré (58, R-5). Open every day

SELF-SERVICE OPÉRA

23 Boulevard des Capucines (127, S-6). Open every day

LIBRE SERVICE MOULIN-ROUGE

92 Boulevard de Clichy (138, D-4). Open every day

LIBRE SERVICE, MAGASINS DU LOUVRE

164 R. de Rivoli (59, V-8). Closed Sundays

LIBRE SERVICE LA SOURCE

35 Boulevard St-Michel (26, O-5). Open every day

LIBRE SERVICE LATIN-CLUNY

98 Boulevard St-Germain (26, P-4). Open every day

Number and letter combinations in parentheses are map references; i.e., "(127, T-5)" means page 127, location T-5.

THE VARIED ATTRACTIONS
OF PARIS NIGHT LIFE

In Paris there is a night spot for every bank roll and taste—from singers and dance bands to nude shows and choirs singing medieval ballads. Minimum or cover charges range from 5 NF at small spots with music, to 15 NF at more elaborate clubs, to 35 NF at top cabarets. Again depending on the place, a bottle of champagne may cost from 35 to 95 NF, a single drink like whisky from 7 to 25 NF.

Small, Lively and Truly French

CAVEAU DES OUBLIETTES
11 Rue St-Julien-le-Pauvre (26, Q-3) ODE 94-97
The Dark Ages are revived in this picturesque *cave*, with its medieval *décor* and ancient, often earthy, folk songs.

CHEZ MA COUSINE
12 Rue Norvins (138, G-2) MON 49-35
Topflight popular singers and tasteful *décor*. The club is at the very top of Montmartre and is worth a visit at night to see the city's lights.

ÉCHELLE DE JACOB
10 Rue Jacob (26, L-2) ODE 53-53. Closed Sundays
A small, pleasant bar where satirical singers make laughter out of the world's folly. These *chansonniers* are a French phenomenon. Unless your French is fluent, the songs won't mean a thing.

ÉCLUSE
15 Quai des Grands-Augustins (26, O-2) No telephone. Closed Mondays
A colorful bar whose small stage has launched many well-known popular singers.

LA GRANDE SÉVERINE
7 Rue St-Séverin (26, P-3) DAN 15-54. Closed Mondays
Ground floor a private club; downstairs an orchestra and dancing in a 12th Century cellar.

LE LAPIN AGILE
4 Rue des Saules (138, G-2) MON 85-87. Closed Mondays
This has been *the* Montmartre *bistro* ever since it was painted by virtually every French artist of the turn of the century. Lapin has a rustic, smoky atmosphere and a blazing log fire on chilly nights. Folk singers entertain; frequently the audience joins in.

MILORD L'ARSOUILLE
5 Rue de Beaujolais (104, B-1) CEN 88-14. Closed Sundays
A cellar club which specializes in topical comedians whose barbs are subtle

Bohemia—with Variations

L'ABBAYE
6 bis Rue de l'Abbaye (26, L-2) ODE 27-77. Closed Sundays
Near Place St-Germain-des-Prés and not far from the Sorbonne, this tiny cabaret often overflows with youth, very much worth observing. If all tables are taken, patrons perch on the piano or bar. Excellent folk singing.

L'ACAPULCO
107 Rue de l'Université (88, L-3) INV 91-96
A Mexican restaurant where audience participation is neither pushy nor cloying. The waiters join in on the more rousing numbers.

even for the French. The atmosphere is jovial, the singers excellent.

AU PORT SALUT
163 bis Rue St-Jacques (26, O-7) ODE 32-03. Closed Mondays
While you wait for food, or for the singers to sing, you can get a "death mask"(actually a life mask) molded on your face.

LA TÊTE DE L'ART
5 Rue de l'Opéra (127, U-10) OPE 53-39. Closed Sundays
Presents some of the town's most expert and intelligent small revues.

CHEZ RÉGINE
1 Rue du Four (26, L-3) DAN 60-70
A small, smoky cellar club with only records for dancing, but this, some experts say, is where the Twist was born.

CLUB ST-GERMAIN-DES-PRÉS
13 Rue St-Benoît (26, K-2) LIT 81-84
A deep, dark cellar hacked out of solid stone in the dead center of the Left Bank's liveliest district. There is jazz and a small dance floor.

CONTRESCARPE
Place de la Contrescarpe (26, R-8) No telephone
This is a uniquely Parisian spot. The

drinks are cheap, the atmosphere easy and the entertainment plentiful. The patrons are colorful and worth study.

KEUR SAMBA
76 Rue de Rennes (26, J-4) LIT 66-30
Once an Existentialist hangout, this is now a semiprivate club with an excellent Latin orchestra for dancing, good food and often good jazz and calypso.

LA POLKA DES MANDIBULES
22 Rue des Cannettes (26, K-4) DAN 42-68

Big and Bare

CRAZY HORSE SALOON
12 Avenue George-V (58, G-6) BAL 69-69
The Crazy Horse's strip-tease acts are as good as any in Paris. The *décor* is an amusing attempt to re-create an American frontier saloon. Jammed every night.

FOLIES PIGALLE
11 Place Pigalle (138, F-5) TRU 25-56
A lavish, flashy show featuring the usual big-cabaret nudity sums up old-time Pigalle. Expensive.

LIDO
78 Avenue des Champs-Élysées (58, J-3) ELY 11-61
Many think the Lido has the best night-club show in the world, blending Amer-

Wine spigots on every table assure the visitor he will not go dry. There is food to go with the wine and entertainment, mainly folk singing.

LE VIEUX-COLOMBIER
21 Rue du Vieux-Colombier (26, J-4) LIT 30-09
Since the death of the great Sidney Bechet, who used to blow his soprano saxophone here, this attractive downstairs room has again become a cabaret, offering on occasion good acts and singers, plus rock-and-roll nights.

ican pace with French taste. Between shows there is dancing for the customers. Good food; moderately expensive.

BAL DU MOULIN ROUGE
*Place Blanche (138, D-4) MON 00-19.
Closed in the winter*
The old Moulin Rouge, made famous by Lautrec's paintings, is now chromium-plated and utterly commercial. However, the specialty of the house, the authentic cancan, is still an exciting number and well worth a look.

LES NATURISTES
*1 Place Pigalle (138, F-5) TRU 13-26.
Closed Sundays*
Naturism, connoting nudity in French, is rife in this Rabelaisian cabaret.

However, the acts and sketches are done with style and wit.

LA NOUVELLE EVE
25 Rue Fontaine (138, E-5) TRI 69-25
Pigalle's neighborhood version of the Lido is short on inventiveness, but still an eye-filling show. Rather expensive.

Cocktail Bars

There are a few "American-style" bars scattered about Paris where the bartender knows, at least in theory, how to make a martini and whisky is served. (Large cafés in central Paris also serve whisky, but the average French café sticks to *apéritifs,* cordials, brandy and beer.) Here is a list of the more interesting American bars.

CALIFORNIA BAR
16 Rue de Berri (58, H-2) ELY 93-00
Rendezvous of foreign correspondents.

CRILLON BAR
Hôtel de Crillon, 10 Place de la Concorde (58, Q-5) ANJ 24-10
The ground-floor bar, convenient to the U.S. Embassy across the street, becomes a headquarters for journalists during international conferences.

LE DRUGSTORE
133 Avenue des Champs-Élysées (58, F-2) BAL 94-40
Besides a bar and restaurant, this wild French version of the American drug-

LE SEXY
68 Rue Pierre-Charron (58, H-4) BAL 25-18
Competes with the Crazy Horse in the new, different and artistic ways in which the girls undress. There are more conventional acts and dancing between the shows.

store has ice cream sundaes, gifts, toys and imported drugs, and makes theater reservations.

HARRY'S NEW YORK BAR
5 Rue Daunou (127, T-7) OPE 73-00
Just off the Place de l'Opéra, Harry's is the most famous American-style bar in Paris. It has been a hangout for Hemingway and other celebrated expatriates, nowadays attracts French newspapermen. There are hot dogs to go with a good glass of tap beer.

LE MONTANA
28 Rue St-Benoît (26, K-2) LIT 93-08
A bar in the center of the St-Germain

des Prés neighborhood which serves a decent martini.

RITZ BAR

Hotel Ritz, Place Vendôme (127, S-8) OPE 28-30. Back entrance, 38 Rue Cambon
A long-time favorite of visiting Americans.

Soft Lights, Sweet Music

LA DOLCE VITA

28 Rue Vavin (26, J-8) LIT 82-45
A small, elegantly done club, where lights are low and dance music is sultry and subdued, plus a truly luxurious touch—telephones at each table to order drinks or call people at the other tables.

DRAP D'OR

58 Rue Bassano (58, G-3) ELY 04-31
A posh spot just off the Champs-Élysées with good singers and dancers.

ÉLÉPHANT BLANC

24 Rue Vavin (26, J-8) ODE 90-95. Closed Sundays
A chic place to dance. Two orchestras keep the music going and help one forget the size of the bill.

EPI-CLUB MONTPARNASSE

132 Boulevard Montparnasse (26, K-10) DAN 50-00
The dancing is to records, the crowd

RELAIS PLAZA

21 Av. Montaigne (58, J-8) BAL 40-96
The street-floor bar, called the Relais, has good drinks and snacks until 2:30 a.m. Downstairs there is the Bar Anglais—no snacks. Both open at 11 a.m. and both are favorites of models—*mannequins*—from nearby fashion houses.

is largely show-business people and very lively. Although officially a private club, it will generally admit any American.

FRANC PINOT

1 Quai de Bourbon (26, S-3) ODE 46-98
On one of the beautiful *quais* of the Île St-Louis, this is the best decorated cellar club in Paris. A place for late dining with an excellent show.

FREDE-CARROLL'S

12 Rue Ste-Anne (127, U-8) RIC 97-86
A very smart spot near the Opéra. The clientele is high-toned, and two orchestras keep the dancing going all night.

MONSEIGNEUR

94 Rue d'Amsterdam (138, B-5) TRI 25-35. Closed Sundays
For years one of the swankiest and most expensive night clubs in the city. A large string orchestra splits up into

small groups. They go wandering about the room serenading the customers.

SHÉHÉRAZADE

3 Rue de Liège (138, C-7) TRI 85-20
Arabian nights *décor* and strolling violinists playing Slavic mood music. A center for celebrities. Expensive.

BLUE NOTE

27 Rue d'Artois (58, J-1) BAL 18-92
This American-owned cabaret provides some of the best quiet jazz in Paris. Bud Powell, the perennial pianist, is often joined by the best jazz players who happen to be passing through town. Dancing. Expensive.

EL CATALAN

16 Rue des Grands-Augustins (26, N-2) DAN 46-07. Closed Mondays
A handsome Spanish restaurant that has a fine Spanish floor show with authentic flamenco music and toe-and-heel dancing.

EL DJAZAIR

27 Rue de la Huchette (26, P-3) ODE 96-97
On the narrow, crooked street Elliott Paul wrote of in *The Last Time I Saw Paris*, this cabaret has the best belly dancing in the city. Excellent rich coffee is served.

VILLA D'ESTE

4 Rue Arsène-Houssaye (58, F-1) ELY 78-44
A small, plush club that persuades well-known singers and comedians to do their acts from midnight to 3 a.m. after they have finished their regular jobs.

Small and Special

THE GASLIGHT CLUB

41 Rue du Colisée (58, L-3) BAL 38-30. Closed Sundays
This is the Paris branch of the private Gaslight Clubs in American cities. Members have keys to the doors of their home clubs. The Paris club will usually open up for visitors and always for American key holders. It resembles a western saloon and has leggy waitresses who sing and dance and try their best to look like the girls in the frontier saloons.

MARS CLUB

6 Rue Robert-Estienne (58, J-4) ELY 47-99
A small bar near the Champs-Élysées that stays open all night for those who have declared war on sleep. It has American-style snacks and drinks, and both French and American jazz singers and players frequently provide the entertainment. The club is also hospitable to Calypso singers.

SONG, DANCE AND PATTER
"À LA PARISIENNE"

At 9 p.m. the curtains go up in the music halls of Paris, and until around midnight the Parisians, a gregarious people who like singing and dancing, enjoy their fill in the traditional home of French vaudeville. The big glossy music halls like the Folies-Bergère surround excellent acts with the most elaborately mounted and extravagantly costumed production numbers in the world. Several smaller halls like the Bobino have small shows rich in Gallic élan and sentiment.

Since its halcyon days before World War I, the music hall as an institution has had its ups and downs. It developed, and prospered with, such great stars as Maurice Chevalier, Mistinguette, Edith Piaf and Yves Montand; it slowly lost these stars and large segments of its clientele to upstart competition—the movies, the tony cabarets, international tours and television. Yet today the big shows and the little ones are in the midst of a modest revival. Here are addresses of theaters that present the best of each kind:

ABC
11 Boulevard Poissonnière (127, Z-6) CEN 19-43. Closed Tuesdays. 12.50 NF top
Recently reconverted to vaudeville after years of musical comedy. Some unusual acts back up the headliners.

ALHAMBRA
50 Rue de Malte (104, P-1) OBE 57-50. Closed Wednesdays. 12.50 NF top
The full name of this large old house is the Alhambra-Maurice Chevalier and here is where that famous entertainer began his career. Usually a music hall, it occasionally reverts to showing films.

BOBINO
20 Rue de la Gaîté (26, F-10) DAN 68-70. Closed Tuesdays. 7.50 NF top
The place to go to get the feel of a small, neighborhood music hall. It often attracts big stars, gets sturdy support from the people of Montparnasse.

CASINO DE PARIS
16 Rue de Clichy (138, C-8) TRI 26-22. Open every evening. 20 NF top
A lavish revue that mixes production numbers, straight acts and soloists. After years of taking a back seat to the Folies-Bergère it is now holding its own in the competition for customers.

THÉÂTRE DE L'ÉTOILE
35 Av. de Wagram (126, F-2) GAL 84-49. Closed Sundays and Mondays. 12.50 NF top
Usually features one-man shows—Yves Montand, Charles Trenet—rather than musical revues. Check before you go.

EUROPÉEN MUSIC-HALL
5 Rue Biot (138, B-4) LAB 53-32. Closed Tuesdays. 15 NF top
Offers as many operettas as it does musical revues.

CONCERT PACRA
10 Bd Beaumarchais (104, P-7) ROQ 48-
78. *Open Fridays, Saturdays, Sundays. 2.50 NF top*
There has been no change in the *décor* here since the turn of the century and the audience is like a group of faithful friends. New acts get a chance and established stars use it as a place to try out new routines.

FOLIES-BERGÈRE
32 Rue Richer (138, J-10) PRO 98-49. Open every evening. 20 NF top
Paris' most famous musical revue. The costumes and sets are as stunning as ever, although the bawdy sketches have been removed, presumably at the request of the French government. However, nudes and near-nudes still abound, often in tableaux which glorify Napoleon and the First Empire.

CONCERT MAYOL
10 Rue de l'Échiquier (127, Z-5) PRO 95-08. Closed Wednesdays. 15 NF top
A small musical revue with emphasis on nudes and earthy sketches.

OLYMPIA
25 Boulevard des Capucines (127, S-6) OPE 25-02. Closed Tuesdays. 15 NF top
An excellent vaudeville house, the first to revive this kind of show after World War II. By presenting new stars it has developed a following among young Parisians.

Number and letter combinations in parentheses are map references; i.e., "(127, T-5)" means page 127, location T-5.

THE THEATER,
MUSIC AND MOVIES

Fluent French is not essential to enjoy Racine or Molière played by the classical troupes; their stylish and graceful performances are treats in themselves. For daily performances, consult the theater section of *Semaine de Paris* or *Paris Weekly Information,* on sale at every newsstand. Curtain time is 8:45 or 9 p.m. The prices are low: good seats at the state theaters cost less than $1; in commercial theaters, under $2.50. Tickets can be bought through your hotel *concierge,* at box offices or through neighborhood ticket agencies.

The State Theater The French government maintains three highly trained theatrical groups in Paris. The purpose of the theaters listed below is to play the classics and, by example, to preserve the purity of spoken French.

COMÉDIE FRANÇAISE, Place du Théâtre Français (*104, B-2*). Matinees on Thursdays, Sundays; closed August.

THÉÂTRE DE FRANCE, Place de l'Odéon (*26, M-5*). Matinees on Thursdays; closed Tuesdays, July-September.

THÉÂTRE NATIONAL POPULAIRE at Palais de Chaillot, Place du Trocadéro (*88, G-2*). This company, directed by Jean Vilar, is in Paris only from mid-November until April, then tours the provinces. Matinees on Thursdays, Saturdays; Sundays, matinee only.

The Commercial Theater This ranges from rollicking farce and gay musicals to witty or somber drama on com-

plicated subjects. French versions of British or American plays, familiar to English-speaking theatergoers, are often available. The Comédie Wagram, listed below, has simultaneous earphone translations into English of the actors' words every night except Tuesdays and Sundays. Most theaters become well known for their specialties—famous authors or actors or styles of play—and try to stick to them. The beauty of the theaters and taste in stage settings are superb. Among the best known of the commercial theaters are:

AMBASSADEURS-HENRI BERNSTEIN, 1 Avenue Gabriel (*58, P-5*)

ATHÉNÉ, Sq. de l'Opéra-L-Jouvet (*127, S-5*) off Rue Caumartin

COMÉDIE DES CHAMPS-ÉLYSÉES, 15 Avenue Montaigne (*58, H-6*)

COMÉDIE WAGRAM, 4 bis Rue de l'Étoile (*126, E-2*)

GAÎTÉ-MONTPARNASSE, 26 Rue de la Gaîté (*26, F-10*)

GYMNASE, 38 Boulevard de Bonne-Nouvelle (*127, Z-6*)

MATHURINS-MARCEL HERRAND, 36 Rue des Mathurins (*126, R-4*)

SARAH BERNHARDT, 1 Place du Châtelet (*104, F-6*)

The Literary Theater Many Paris theaters have distinctive reputations as literary theaters. This is because of the consistently high literary quality of their productions, as at the Vieux Colombier, or because they are favored by an important playwright—Jean-Paul Sartre at the Antoine—or because they develop new talent. Among them are:

ANTOINE, 14 Boulevard de Strasbourg (*138, O-10*)

L'ATELIER, Place Charles-Dullin (*138, H-4*)

HUCHETTE, 23 Rue de la Huchette (*26, P-3*)

MONTPARNASSE-GASTON BATY, 31 Rue de la Gaîté (*26, F-10*)

OEUVRE, 55 Rue de Clichy (*138, C-6*)

POCHE MONTPARNASSE, 75 Bd du Montparnasse (*26, G-8*)

STUDIO DES CHAMPS-ÉLYSÉES, 13 Avenue Montaigne (*58, H-6*)

VIEUX COLOMBIER, 21 Rue du Vieux-Colombier (*26, J-4*)

A Special Theater World renowned among devotees of the most horrible horror is the Grand Guignol, 20 bis Rue Chaptal (*138, D-6*). This theater offers two acts nightly in which arms will be torn from shoulders, blood will flow in buckets and the characters will talk in eerie screams. These are topped off with two fast acts of soothing bedroom farce.

Sound of Music Opera is at its best at the Opéra itself, Place de l'Opéra (*127, T-5*); closed Tuesdays, Thursdays and during August; ballet on Wednesdays (*pages 132-133*). But opera can also be seen at the Opéra Comique, 5 Rue Favart (*127, W-6*); closed Mondays, Tuesdays and during July. Often these companies present the same opera, and the only real distinction is that the Opéra is large and magnificent, the Opéra Comique smaller and more intimate. Next in musical importance come the Palais de Chaillot, Place du Trocadéro (*88, G-2*), which besides the plays of the Théâtre National Populaire also presents concerts and ballet; the three auditoriums in the huge Théâtre des Champs-Élysées, 15 Avenue Montaigne (*58, H-6*); the Salle Pleyel, one large and two small (Salles Chopin and Debussy) auditoriums, 252 Rue du Faubourg-St-Honoré (*126, G-2*); the Salle Gaveau's two auditoriums, 45 Rue La Boétie (*126, M-4*). To discover what is available on any particular day consult *Semaine de Paris* under Music and Opera, or the entertainment columns of any of the daily newspapers.

The Movies The French movie world centers on 18 de luxe movie theaters scattered around the Champs-Élysées area. The best of everything, native or foreign, comes here first. These theaters usually show the foreign films in the language in which they were made, and newspaper advertisements will read "V.O." for *version originale*. Thus American and British films will be played in English. But it is also fun to visit a neighborhood movie house and listen to the dubbed version of an American western in French.

For the Youngsters Besides zoos and puppets in the parks (*page 195*) there are circuses, and special plays for children are given at Thursday matinees in some of the theaters.

CIRQUE D'HIVER, 110 Rue Amelot (*104, P-2*). Programs change monthly.

CIRQUE MÉDRANO, 63 Boulevard Rochechouart (*138, H-5*)

CIRQUE DE FRANCE, Pte de Versailles (*Paris map, front end paper, E-9*)

TRAVELING CIRCUSES appear from time to time; watch the newspapers.

THÉÂTRE DES ENFANTS MODÈLES, Salle Chopin-Pleyel, 252 Rue du Faubourg-St-Honoré (*126, G-2*)

THÉÂTRE DU PETIT MONDE (Théâtre de l'A.B.C.), 11 Boulevard Poissonnière (*127, Z-6*)

THÉÂTRE DES ENFANTS (Théâtre de la Porte St-Martin), 6 Bd St-Martin (*Paris map, front end paper, L-4*)

Number and letter combinations in parentheses are map references; i.e., "(127, T-5)" means page 127, location T-5.

THE ART AND JOY
OF SHOPPING IN PARIS

Shopping in Paris is not for the faint of heart, the footsore or the ferocious bargain-seeker. It is rather a special enjoyment, like a French meal, and should not be approached as a reckless foray the morning one's plane is leaving. (However, if you are having a wonderful time, and put off shopping till the last minute, there are plenty of shops that stock small handsome items.) The best Paris bargains are often the most expensive. They are mostly things produced by hand, in small quantities, by old-world methods. They are bargains because only France has the skills and knowledge that go into them, and their high price will be lower than it would be at home after shipping charges and markups are added. Don't be surprised if some shopkeepers treat you with chilling indifference. It's part of the shopping adventure, and a scornful salesgirl can scare even a Parisian. Good advice is to shop as you would in any large city—with one careful eye out for values and the other on your budget. Many stores give discounts if you pay in traveler's checks. And European editions of English-language papers print latest information on sales, auctions and special offerings.

The Best Buys Custom-made women's dresses and ready-to-wear hats, accessories and knitted dresses top the list. They are expensive but worth the money. Remember, too, that shopping takes time as well as money. Men can find superb ties and gloves and custom shirts and robes. Other items worth looking for but not cheap are fine leather goods (handbags, gloves, luggage and accessories); jewelry, real and unreal; antiques; original prints, drawings and paintings; books; decorative objects and gadgets, both ancient and modern. The perfumes and brandies, which cost more than twice as much in the United States, are real bargains.

Shopping Services These can save your life if you don't like doing your own buying. There are special shops that will deliver anything from caviar to cameras to your plane or boat, and experienced shoppers who will take over your entire list of chores. You can even do this by phone, leaving selection to them. Here are a few names of such services:

SHOPPERS Mrs. John Lithiby, Chez Jansen, 9 Rue Royale, ANJ 65-35; Lillian de Lignante, 1 Rue Magellan, BAL 36-98; Laura Bacon Suggests, 8 Place Vendôme, OPE 10-03
SHOPS Société des Produits Euro-péens, 6 Square de l'Opéra-L-Jouvet and 22 Rue de Caumartin, OPE 76-18; Chunn (perfumes), 43 Rue Richer, TAI 42-06; Michel Swiss, 16 Rue de la Paix, OPE 64-52; Helene Dale, 7 Rue Scribe, OPE 92-60

Last-Minute Shopping This can still be accomplished by desperate travelers at the quick-service stores at Orly airport, after checking in for the flight back home. If you are traveling by sea, you can take good advantage of the shops on board to select from the wide varieties they stock.

American Customs Regulations A customs man, usually pleasant, will be among the first Americans to welcome you back on home soil. The duty-free limit on foreign purchases is now $100 per person. There is a limit of five bottles (fifths) of liquor duty-free and one bottle of each of most kinds of perfume. The duty varies widely on different kinds of goods, which is a factor to consider when you are bargain-hunting in Paris. Antique furniture (pre-1830) or original works of art, for example, are not cheap to buy or to ship, but they are duty-free and the markup on such items is high at home. Don't forget to itemize on your declaration the things you are having shipped to you. Remember duty is generally figured on wholesale price; dealers will usually supply this, or customs men will make an estimate. The customs inspector will help you to get the high-duty items in under your duty-free quota. Sample rates:

U.S. Duty Charges

CLOTHING Dresses, suits: 21-42 per cent; gloves: 35 per cent; leather goods: 20 per cent; neckties: 32 per cent; unornamented umbrellas: 20 per cent

HOUSEHOLD Cutlery: 15 per cent; furniture: 10-17 per cent; glassware: 30-50 per cent; unembroidered table and bed linen: 10-12 per cent; china: 35 per cent

JEWELRY Unset stones: about 10 per cent; costume jewelry: 55 per cent; gold jewelry (with stones): 30 per cent; pearls: 5 per cent, strung with a clasp: 55 per cent

MISCELLANEOUS Dolls: 35-38 per cent; phonograph records: 12 per cent; toys: 21-44 per cent; cigarette lighters: 30-45 per cent; silk and wool fabrics: 21-32½ per cent

Gift Parcels Under-$10 parcels help boost the number of things you can buy in Paris despite the $100 duty-free limit. Gifts you mail home (except for perfume and liquor) are not counted in your total duty-free allowance provided the total worth of each parcel is not more than $10. (Stores usually figure a wholesale value, so you can spend $12 or $14 and still be under $10.) You cannot send more than one parcel per day to the same person at one address. You can mail very light items like scarves and gloves in an envelope. Surface mail is much the cheapest but takes at least a couple of weeks. Let stores send breakable items; their packaging will generally assure a safe arrival.

Mailing Packages Home This is simple if they are small and you know the rules. You can do it yourself or get your hotel *concierge* to do it. You, or a shop, can mail a parcel up to 500 grams (1.1 pounds) out of France by marking it *échantillons* (samples). This assures French Customs that it has no commercial value. For the benefit of U.S. Customs it should also be marked: "GIFT—Value under $10." Slightly bigger items—up to a limit of one kilo (2.2 pounds)—are called *petits paquets* (little packages) and can also be mailed, at somewhat higher postage. In theory you can mail parcels weighing up to 24 pounds, but if your shopping has gotten this far out of hand you'd better turn it over to a professional shipper who gets paid well for doing the dirty work. If you are returning by ship and don't mind climbing on the boat train with an end table or a rocking chair, you can afford to pay less attention to weight when you shop.

THE HEADY PLEASURES
OF SHOPPING FOR CLOTHES

Department Stores   Roughly grouped in the center of the city on the Right Bank, Paris' department stores are large and well stocked. They are good for notions and necessities, perfumes and some clothing, but you'll have to look elsewhere for de luxe Parisian items. Amateur chefs can have a wonderful time shopping for kitchen gadgets at Printemps and Galeries Lafayette. All department stores have large stocks of children's clothes much to American taste. The huge Grands Magasins du Louvre, full of moderately priced wares, is a convenient place to shop for last-minute souvenirs. Some addresses:

AU PRINTEMPS, 64 Boulevard Haussmann (*127, S-4*)

AUX TROIS QUARTIERS, 17 Boulevard de la Madeleine (*126, R-7*)

GALERIES LAFAYETTE, 38-46 Boulevard Haussmann (*127, T-4*)

GRANDS MAGASINS DU LOUVRE, Place du Palais-Royal (*59, V-8*)

LA GRANDE MAISON DE BLANC, 8 Boulevard des Capucines (*127, U-6*)

SAMARITAINE DE LUXE, 27 Boulevard des Capucines (*127, T-6*)

Women's sizes: French and U.S. equivalents

BLOUSES, SWEATERS, LINGERIE						DRESSES, SUITS, COATS						
FRANCE	40	42	44	46	48	**FRANCE**	38	40	42	44	46	48
U.S.		32	34	36	38	40	**U.S.**		10	12	14	16	18	20

"Haute Couture"   Buying a dress from one of the great Paris fashion houses is a woman's ultimate shopping experience, but it takes money (a dress can easily cost $500) and four weeks for fittings. Book your seat for showings in advance through your *concierge* or by phone. Take along your passport to prove you aren't a fashion pirate and wear your best suit. Many of the big houses now have delightful *boutiques*, with less expensive ready-to-wear or semi-custom clothes. Here are some top *haute couture* addresses:

BALENCIAGA, 10 Avenue George-V (*58, G-6*) BAL 98-70

BALMAIN, 44 Rue François-I (*58, H-4*) BAL 68-40

CHANEL, 31 Rue Cambon (*58, S-4*) OPE 60-21

PIERRE CARDIN, 118 Rue du Fbg-St-Honoré (*126, N-5*) BAL 06-23

JEAN DESSÈS, 17 Avenue Matignon (*58, M-3*) BAL 45-63

CHRISTIAN DIOR, 30 Avenue Montaigne (*58, J-6*) ELY 93-64

GIVENCHY, 3 Avenue George-V (*58, G-6*) BAL 92-60

JACQUES HEIM, 15 Av. Matignon; teen shop: No. 11 (*58, M-3*) ELY 62-23

LANVIN-CASTILLO, 22 Rue du Fbg-St-Honoré (*126, Q-7*) ANS 27-21

GUY LAROCHE, 29 Avenue Montaigne (*58, J-5*) BAL 57-66

NINA RICCI, 20 Rue des Capucines (*127, S-7*) OPE 67-31

CLAUDE RIVIÈRE, 75 Rue du Fbg-St-Honoré (*126, N-5*) ELY 40-49

Smaller Dress Shops   These little stores are less expensive than the big houses. They carry some chic ready-to-wear clothes, and alterations are generally free, but the best buys are the things you have made to order. Some addresses:

ANNA LOWE, 35 Avenue Matignon (*58, N-2*)

ANNY BLATT, 27 Boulevard Malesherbes (*126, Q-5*)

HENRY À LA PENSÉE, 5 Rue du Fbg-St-Honoré (*126, Q-7*)

JACQUES ESTEREL, 85 bis Rue du Fbg-St-Honoré (*126, M-5*)

JAMIQUA, 6 Rue Marbeuf (*58, H-5*)

JANE THEVENON, 20 Rue Royale (*58, R-4*)

JEAN DESTRE, 15 Rue Daunou (*127, T-6*)

WALLIS, 63 Avenue des Champs-Élysées (*58, J-3*)

BORGIA, 58 Rue Pierre-Charron (*58, H-4*)

JOUVIN, 1 bis R. Auber (*127, T-5*)

MORABITO, 346 Rue St-Honoré (*127, S-8*)

SAGAN, 4 Pl. Vendôme (*127, S-8*)

Blouses and Lingerie

Prices may seem high by American standards, and again the best buys may be the made-to-order things. There are a number of elegant shops along the Rue du Faubourg-St-Honoré. Other addresses:

BERLÉ, 14 Rue Clément-Marot (*58, H-5*)

DOUCET JEUNE, 10 Rue Halévy (*127, T-5*)

MONY, 33 Av. de l'Opéra (*127, U-8*)

LECADRE-MARNIER, 25 Rue du Fbg-St-Honoré (*126, P-7*)

LUCYLE VALÉRY, 10 Rue du Mont-Thabor (*59, S-6*)

PACHE, 6 R. de Castiglione (*59, S-6*)

Gloves and Handbags

Cheap French gloves and leather handbags are not worth bringing home. But if you shop for workmanship and quality, they are among the best buys in France. (See Leather Goods, page 184.) It is best to get the *lavable* (washable) leather gloves. Some addresses:

ARIS, 83 Rue du Fbg-St-Honoré (*126, M-5*)

HERMÉS, 24 Rue du Fbg-St-Honoré (*126, Q-7*)

Children's Clothes, Toys

These turn out to be more expensive than you expect, except in the department stores. But some of the children's shops have tempting items with a particularly Parisian look to them. Among the best-known stores:

Clothes

ENFANTILLAGE, 60 Boulevard de Courcelles (*126, K-1*)

VIRGINIE, 168 Rue du Fbg-St-Honoré (*126, K-4*)

Toys

À LA DAUPHINE, 49 Quai des Grands-Augustins (*26, O-2*)

AU NAIN BLEU, 408 Rue St-Honoré (*126, R-7*)

Men's clothes

Men do better in Paris for their women than for themselves. However, there are enough haberdashers and custom tailors to let a man indulge himself. Some addresses:

DORIAN GUY, 36 Avenue George-V (*58, G-4*)

HILDRITCH & KEY, 252 Rue de Rivoli (*126, R-8*)

LANVIN FOR MEN, 15 Rue du Fbg-St-Honoré (*126, Q-7*)

MADELIOS, 10 Place de la Madeleine (*126, R-6*)

POIRIER, 12 Rue Boissy-d'Anglas (*126, Q-7*)

SULKA, 2 Rue de Castiglione (*59, S-6*)

Jewelry Costume jewelry is a Paris specialty, but duty (often 55 per cent) and prices are high. Antique jewelry is expensive and hard to find. Visitors who window-shop jewelers like Cartier at 12 Rue de la Paix (*127, T-7*) and Van Cleef and Arpels at 22 Place Vendôme (*127, S-8*) often settle for something less expensive at shops such as:

BOUCHERON (fine jewelry), 26 Place Vendôme (*127, S-7*)

MME NOELLA RIOTTEAU (fine jewelry), 22 Place Vendôme (*127, S-8*)

M. GUSTAVE (values in old jewelry), 416 Rue St-Honoré (*127, R-7*)

COUNTESS ZOLOWSKA (costume jewelry), 9 Quai Malaquais (*89, Z-5*)

Perfume Always insist on labeled, sealed bottles, and stick to reputable stores. You find perfume in department stores, drugstores and gift stores and in the *haute couture boutiques* or at the maker's showroom. Guerlain sells its scents only in its own stores. Some addresses:

CARON, 10 Place Vendôme (*127, S-8*)

GUERLAIN, 2 Place Vendôme and 68 Av. des Champs-Élysées (*127, S-8*)

COTY, 27 Place Vendôme (*127, S-7*)

LE DRUGSTORE, 133 Avenue des Champs-Élysées (*58, F-2*)

ELIZABETH ARDEN, 7 Place Vendôme (*127, S-8*)

RONYL, 52-60 Avenue des Champs-Élysées (*58, J-3*)

Leather Goods Together with the stores listed under Gloves and Handbags (*page 183*), the shops listed here offer everything in leather from elegant billfolds to luggage.

AU DÉPART, 29 Avenue de l'Opéra (*127, U-8*)

LOUIS VUITTON, 78 bis Avenue Marceau (*58, F-3*)

LA PEAU DE PORC, 2 bis Rue Caumartin (*126, S-6*)

SCHILZ, 30 Rue Caumartin (*127, S-5*)

For the Table In this high-duty category, sacrifice quantity to buy quality—Baccarat and Lalique glass, Sèvres and Limoges china, French bed and table linens. Among the best shops are:

BACCARAT (crystal), 30 bis Rue de Paradis (*138, M-9*)

PORTHAULT (linen), 18 R. de la Grange-Batelière (*127, X-4*)

LALIQUE (crystal), 11 Rue Royale (*126, Q-7*)

ROUARD (china), 34 Avenue de l'Opéra (*127, U-7*)

Food and Liquor Your one-gallon (five fifths) duty-free allowance of spirits is best filled with brandies, which cost two thirds less in France than in the U.S. All kinds of brandy and gourmet delicacies will recall Paris back at home. They may be had at the following fine shops (some are open Sunday mornings; all are closed Mondays):

FAUCHON, 26 and 28 Place de la Madeleine (*126, R-6*)

HÉDIARD, 21 Place de la Madeleine (*126, R-6*)

ANDROUËT (for cheeses), 41 Rue d'Amsterdam (*126, R-1*)

CORCELLET, 18 Avenue de l'Opéra (*127, U-8*)

BATTENDIER, 8 Rue Coquillière (*104, E-2*)

BONHOURS, 56 Rue François I (*58, H-4*)

Antiques If you know antiques, you can bring home some of the best buys in Paris. The Flea Market is good (*pages 148-149*), but not as cheap as it used to be. The Village Suisse, open Thursdays until midnight, closed Tuesdays and Wednesdays (*88, K-5*), near the Eiffel Tower, is one rung up and a good place to find French provincial plates, copper and brass. Right Bank dealers around the Place Beauvau have stocks fit for museums—and prices to match. Probably your best hunting ground is on the Left Bank in a square mile based on the Quai Voltaire (closed Saturdays or Mondays, open Wednesday nights until 11) where you may just find a moderately priced prize. Visit the weekday auctions (closed in August) at the Hôtel Drouot, 9 Rue Drouot (*127, X-5*); here professionals will bid for you for a percentage fee. No matter where or what you buy, try to get written on your receipt the dealer's estimate of the age of each piece. (U.S. customs says an article must be pre-1830 to be an antique.) Some addresses, out of hundreds:

Right Bank

DUGRENOT (decorator items), 107 Rue du Fbg-St-Honoré (*126, M-5*)

ÉTIENNE LEVY (fine general selection), 178 Rue du Fbg-St-Honoré (*126, K-4*)

JANSEN (fine furniture, top prices), 9 Rue Royale (*126, Q-8*)

SELIGMANN (17-18th Century items), 23 Place Vendôme (*127, S-8*)

Left Bank

LES COURTINES DE LISETTE (curios), 12 Rue de Beaune (*89, X-4*)

GILBERT SUC (bric-a-brac), 30 Rue des Saints-Pères (*89, Y-6*)

CHEZ JOSÉPHINE, 1 Rue Bonaparte (*26, L-1*)

TOUZAIN (18th Century *objets d'art*), 27 Quai Voltaire (*89, X-4*)

Prints and Paintings Art is duty-free, and despite rising prices there are still excellent values to be had, especially in prints; you may even find a lithograph by Picasso for about $100. But important prints are sky-high. In painting, you can find a pleasant water color for as little as a few dollars. Any purchase of $500 or more requires a permit (and, if you're in any doubt, the opinion of an outside expert). Make sure the gallery does all the legal work or you'll be at it for weeks. Do not overlook the Louvre's excellent original prints and reproductions, which are sold on both the ground floor and first floor. Some reliable addresses:

BERGGRUEN & CIE., 70 Rue de l'Université (*89, W-5*)

MAEGHT GALLERY, 13 Rue de Tehéran (*126, M-2*)

BRÉHÉRET & PRAT, Quai Malaquais, corner R. Bonaparte (*26, L-1*)

GALERIE DE FRANCE, 3 Rue du Fbg-St-Honoré (*126, Q-7*)

BRAUN, 18 Rue Louis-le-Grand (*127, U-6*)

LA MAISON DE LA PENSÉE FRAN-ÇAISE, 2 Rue de l'Élysée (*58, O-4*)

Books Old or new, French books are duty-free and easily mailable. Art books are magnificent and dear. For old books, browse through the antiquarian shops on the Rue Bonaparte (*26, L-1*) and near the university. Some addresses:

BRENTANO'S (for new books), 37 Avenue de l'Opéra (*127, U-7*)

FLAMMARION (new French titles), 36 bis Avenue de l'Opéra (*127, U-7*)

GALIGNANI'S (wide selection), 224 Rue de Rivoli (*127, S-9*)

SIMONE BARBIER (books on Paris), 14 Rue de l'Université (*89, Y-5*)

MUSEUMS,
GREAT AND MINOR

The French concern for the arts, science, literature and history is best displayed in Paris' museums. Here are preserved not only masterpieces of craft and intellect but also the memorabilia of some of the great men who helped create world civilization. Except as noted, museums are closed on Tuesdays and holidays. The admission is usually only 1 NF.

The Great Museums of Art

MUSÉE DU LOUVRE
(*Pages 60-73*)

MUSÉE DU JEU DE PAUME
(*Pages 74-75*)

MUSÉE DE L'ORANGERIE
Jardin des Tuileries (58, Q-7)
These beautiful showrooms are used for important temporary art exhibitions, announced in the newspapers.
• *Highlight:* two rooms decorated with Claude Monet's giant *Nymphéas.*

MUSÉE NATIONAL D'ART MODERNE
*13 Avenue du Président-Wilson (88, L-1).
Open 10-5*
A rich display of 20th Century art and special rooms containing work by such

great artists as Bonnard, Utrillo, Rouault, Matisse, Picasso.

MUSÉE MUNICIPAL D'ART MODERNE
*11 Avenue du Président-Wilson (88, L-1).
Open 10-12, 2-6*
Adjacent to the Musée National d'Art Moderne, the museum comprises rooms rented for exhibitions as well as a permanent exhibition of modern paintings.

PETIT-PALAIS
Avenue Alexandre-III (58, N-6). Open 10-5 except when major exhibitions are being prepared
Built for the World's Fair of 1900, now the Fine Arts Museum of the City of Paris. Here is housed French art from the Middle Ages to the 18th Century.

Other Art Museums

MUSÉE DES ARTS DÉCORATIFS
107 Rue de Rivoli (59, V-8). Open 10-12, 2-5
This museum celebrates the "minor arts" of decoration, boasts a huge collection of home furnishings.

MUSÉE JACQUEMART-ANDRÉ
158 Boulevard Haussmann (126, L-3). Generally open 1-6, varying with the exhibition
This typical mansion of Haussmann's day has paintings by such 18th Century French painters as Watteau, works of Rubens and Rembrandt, art and furniture of the Italian Renaissance.
• *Highlight:* the finest Tiepolo in France, a fresco of Henri III arriving in Venice.

MUSÉE COGNACQ-JAY
25 Boulevard des Capucines (127, T-6). Open 10-12, 2-5
Displayed here are the art collections (mostly 18th Century) of Ernest Cognacq-Jay, self-made businessman and philanthropist.
• *Highlight:* the first known painting by Rembrandt, *Balaam's Ass.*

MUSÉE NISSIM-DE-CAMONDO
63 Rue de Monceau (126, M-1). Open 2-5 daily, Sundays 10-12; closed July 14-September 15

A fine collection of 18th Century furniture and art, displayed with elegance and excellent taste.
• *Highlights:* splendid tapestries of Aubusson and Beauvais; a collection of Chinese porcelains.

MUSÉE DE CÉRAMIQUE (DE SÈVRES)
4 Grande Rue, Sèvres (Environs map, front end paper, G-6). Open 10-5
An enormous array of ceramics housed about eight miles from Paris on the route to Versailles. It presents a vivid history of the "arts of fire," ceramic objects gathered from the world over.
• *Highlight:* beautiful *biscuit,* or twice-baked, porcelain.

MUSÉE CERNUSCHI
7 Avenue Velasquez (126, M-1). Open 10-6 April-September, 10-5 October-March
Ancient Oriental art in luxurious 19th Century settings. Around a huge Japanese bronze Buddha are grouped a variety of ceramics, jades, bronzes and paintings.

MUSÉE GUIMET
6 Place d'Iéna (88, J-1). Open 10-5
Works from India, Indonesia, China, Tibet, Japan and Afghanistan make this the best ensemble of Asian art in the western world.

MUSÉE RODIN

*77 Rue de Varenne (89, S-6). Open 1-6
March 16-October 15, 1-5 October 16-March
15*
Erected in 1731, this building now honors the sculptor Rodin, who lived and worked here. It has many of his bronzes and marbles, including such famous works as *The Kiss*. In the courtyard stands this master sculptor's *Gate of Hell* with replicas of many of the major sculptures he created.

MUSÉE EUGÈNE DELACROIX

6 R. de Furstenberg (26, L-2). Open 10-5
Delacroix's home in his last years, this museum contains drawings, water colors and a few canvases by the artist, as well as memorabilia of his life.

MUSÉE BOURDELLE

*16 Rue Antoine-Bourdelle (26, D-9). Open
10-12, 2-5*
A great many sculptures and paintings by Bourdelle, Rodin's protégé.

Museums of History

MUSÉE DE L'HISTOIRE DE FRANCE

*60 Rue des Francs-Bourgeois (104, K-4).
Open 2-5*
Displayed in elegant rococo salons of the Hôtel de Soubise documents from the Archives Nationales trace 12 centuries of France's history from the Merovingians of the Middle Ages up to

MUSÉE GUSTAVE MOREAU

*14 Rue La Rochefoucauld (127, U-2). Open
10-5; closed Sundays*
A cluttered, bizarre private mansion that is a rich storehouse of Moreau's paintings, drawings and studies.

MUSÉE BALZAC

47 Rue Raynouard (88, D-6). Open 1-5
Miniature models of characters in Balzac's novels, portraits of the author, cartoons and keepsakes fill this small house, once Balzac's tightly locked retreat from his creditors.

MUSÉE VICTOR HUGO

*6 Place des Vosges (104, 0-7). Open 10-12
and 2-5:30 April-September, 10-12 and
2-5 October-March*
Victor Hugo lived here for 16 years, writing some of his finest works. There are documents and works by his artist friends, including Delacroix and Carpeaux, and nearly 400 interesting drawings by Hugo himself.

1848 and the downfall of Louis-Philippe.
• *Highlight:* the private diary of Louis XVI, whose sole entry for the fateful date of July 14, 1789, was "nothing."

MUSÉE DES MONUMENTS FRANÇAIS

Palais de Chaillot (88, G-2). Open 10-5
All the phases of French sculpture and

France's worldly and religious architecture are represented by actual-size replicas of details of many impressive buildings, as well as miniature replicas of important monuments and churches.

MUSÉE DE CLUNY

*6 Place Paul-Painlevé (26, P-5). Open 10-
12:45, 2-5*
Devoted mainly to the works of the Middle Ages, this museum shows beautiful statuary from ancient cathedrals, Byzantine ivories and jewels. Here are the monumental Gallo-Roman ruins of the Thermae (baths) dating from the 3rd Century, when Paris was called Lutèce.
• *Highlight:* the outstanding *Lady with the Unicorn* tapestries.

MUSÉE CARNAVALET

(Pages 118-119)

Museums of French Culture and Costume

MUSÉE DES ARTS ET
TRADITIONS POPULAIRES

Palais de Chaillot (88, G-2). Open 10-5
A museum of French folklore. Temporary exhibitions, display types of dwellings, costumes, handicrafts, games.

MUSÉE DU COSTUME

*11 Avenue du Président-Wilson (88, L-1).
Open 10-12, 2-6 including holidays*
More than 5,000 gowns on display here

MUSÉE DE L'ARMÉE

(Pages 102-103)

CABINET DES MÉDAILLES
ET ANTIQUITÉS

*Bibliothèque Nationale, 58 Rue de Richelieu (127, W-8). Open 10-12, 2-4; closed
Sundays and during Easter time*
Greek and Roman statuary, 400,000 coins from every western civilization and the world's largest collection of cameos. Don't be put off by the enormous iron gate that bars the entrance; ring the bell, and a guard will let you in.

MUSÉE DES PLANS-RELIEFS

*Hôtel des Invalides (88, R-4). Open 10-12,
2-5:30*
A unique collection of replicas in the Hôtel des Invalides dating from the time of Louis XIV that show towns, castles, harbors and scenes of France.

offer a history (since 1725) of the skills of the *couturiers.*

MUSÉE DE L'OPÉRA

*Place Charles-Garnier (127, T-6). Open
10-5; closed Sundays*
In the Opéra building are souvenirs of composers and celebrated performers, models of stage designs and costumes, works of Delacroix and Renoir, original ballet and opera scores.

Number and letter combinations in parentheses are map references; i.e., "(127, T-5)" means page 127, location T-5.

Museums of Science

MUSÉE DU CONSERVATOIRE NATIONAL DES ARTS ET MÉTIERS
292 Rue St-Martin (104, J-1). Open 1:30-5:30 weekdays, 10-5 Sundays; closed Mondays
A museum devoted to the history of mechanical invention throughout the world. It occupies what used to be the Church of St-Martin-des-Champs.
• *Highlight:* the airplane in which Blériot first flew the Channel in 1909. Splendid mechanical exhibits that tell the history of clockworks.

MUSÉUM NATIONAL D'HISTOIRE NATURELLE
57 Rue Cuvier (27, U-8). Open 1:30-5 weekdays, 10:30-5 Sundays
A botanical garden, a zoo (*page 195*), a gallery of natural history, all crowded within the Jardin des Plantes.

MUSÉE DE L'HOMME
(Pages 102-103)

MUSÉE DE LA MARINE
(Pages 100-101)

Museums for the Specialist

Further information on these and other special museums may be obtained from the Paris Welcome Information Office, 7 Rue Balzac, ELY 52-78, and the National Office for Tourist Information, 127 Avenue des Champs-Élysées, BAL 12-80.

MUSÉE DU CINÉMA
82 Rue de Courcelles (126, J-1)
The history of films.

MUSÉE DE LA MONNAIE
11 Quai de Conti (26, M-1)
The history of French currency.

MUSÉE DE LA PRÉFECTURE DE POLICE
36 Quai des Orfèvres (26, Q-2)
Police history and the Resistance of World War II.

MUSÉE POSTAL
4 Rue St-Romain (26, E-6)
Postage stamps, mailboxes carried by horse or mule, documents.

MUSÉE DE L'ART JUIF
12 Rue des Saules (138, G-1)
Jewish art.

CONSERVATOIRE NATIONAL DE MUSIQUE ET DE DÉCLAMATION
14 Rue de Madrid (126, P-1)
Musical instruments, including those of Marie-Antoinette, Ludwig van Beethoven, Jean-Baptiste Lully.

HISTORIC BUILDINGS THAT CROWN A METROPOLIS

Most of the buildings on this page can be visited, others can only be seen from the street, but all are important to the story of Paris. You may be lucky enough to see some in their pristine state—in 1960 the government embarked on a project to scrub grime from the city's monuments, a project that has set off a raging controversy among traditionalists.

Government and Historical

THE CONCIERGERIE
(Pages 38-39)

HÔTEL LAMBERT
2 Rue St-Louis-en-l' Île (27, U-4)
Designed by the architect Le Vau, this mansion was erected in 1640. The rooms, decorated by the painters Le Brun and Le Sueur, were once inhabited by Voltaire and his mistress. Don't overlook the facade if you are touring the Île St-Louis. Unfortunately, the interior can be visited only twice a year by special permission.

HÔTEL DE LAUZUN
17 Quai d'Anjou (27, U-4) GUT 05-41. Visits arranged by the Service of Historic Monuments, 3 Rue de Valois
First inhabited by the gallant duke whose name it bears, this handsome mansion also housed in 1847 the writers Baudelaire and Gautier.

HÔTEL DE SENS
1 Rue du Figuier (104, L-8). Open 1:30-8:30 Tuesdays through Fridays
This building and the Musée de Cluny are two superb examples of medieval residential architecture in Paris. This is in the Gothic style called Flamboyant, and restoration was started in 1936.

HÔTEL DE VILLE
(Pages 114-115)

PALAIS BOURBON
(Pages 90-91)

PALAIS DE L'ÉLYSÉE
55 Rue du Faubourg-St-Honoré (58, O-3).
Closed to the public
The home of French presidents since 1873, the Élysée Palace has become a center of government activity under the Fifth Republic.

PALAIS DE JUSTICE
(Pages 38-39)

PALAIS DE LA LÉGION D'HONNEUR
64 Rue de Lille (89, V-3).
Open 2-5 Thursdays and Saturdays
Once the residence of Mme de Staël, since 1804 the building has been the home of the Legion of Honor. It con-

tains a museum of medals, documents and paintings.

PALAIS DU LUXEMBOURG
15 Rue de Vaugirard (26, M-5)
Visits on Sundays permitted with written authorization of the Secrétariat Général de la Questure du Sénat
Built for Queen Marie de Médicis, this palace is the seat of the Senate (the upper house of the French parliament).

PALAIS-ROYAL
(Pages 106-107)

PANTHÉON
(Pages 48-49)

Institutions of Learning

BIBLIOTHÈQUE HISTORIQUE DE LA VILLE DE PARIS
29 Rue de Sévigné (104, N-5).
Open 9:30-12, 1:30-5 except Sundays
This library contains over 400,000 volumes pertaining to the history of Paris and the Revolution.

BIBLIOTHÈQUE NATIONALE
58 Rue de Richelieu (127, W-8). Open 9-6 except Sundays and holidays; get admission card at entrance
In this handsome building are housed more than six million books, five million prints, 136,000 volumes of manuscripts and 300,000 maps. It shares

honors with the British Museum as the world's largest library.

ÉCOLE DES BEAUX-ARTS
14 Rue Bonaparte (26, L-1)
Although most famous for its costume balls, this is a serious school of art. In the courtyards are the doorway of the Château of Anet (1547) and the front of the Château of Gaillon (1500).

ÉCOLE MILITAIRE
Avenue de La Motte-Picquet (88, O-9).
Visits by application only
The École Militaire has been training young men in the art of warfare since

1759. It owes its existence to the efforts of a financier and Mme de Pompadour.

INSTITUT DE FRANCE
23 Quai de Conti (26, M-1). Permission for Saturday and Sunday visits required from Directeur des Services Administratifs, 23 Quai de Conti
This is the home of the "Immortals,"

LA BOURSE
Place de la Bourse (127, X-7). Only male visitors admitted
This 19th Century neoclassical building, based on the Roman temple of Vespasian, is the stock exchange. The most active hours are between 11 a.m. and 3 p.m. when its hall, the Parquet, is jammed with stockbrokers.

PALAIS DE LA DÉFENSE
Rond-Point de la Défense, Puteaux (Paris map, front end paper, A-2)
The huge modern edifice with a roof like an overturned shell encompasses an area of more than 980,000 square feet and is used for international technical exhibitions and congresses.

GRAND-PALAIS
Avenue Alexandre-III (58, M-6). Open 10-12, 2-5 except Fridays
Built for the Exposition of 1900, the

the 40 members of the Académie Française, who labor one hour each week putting out a dictionary whose deadline is 70 years off. Four other academies also sit here. The Institut also contains the famous Mazarine library.

THE SORBONNE
(Pages 44-45)

Miscellaneous

Grand-Palais is used for various exhibitions. The western part is the Palais de la Découverte, a science museum.

NATO HEADQUARTERS
Place du Maréchal de Lattre-de-Tassigny (150, R-10)
Within this A-shaped building, opened in 1959, are 1,000 offices of NATO. The NATO Council has public sessions.

PALAIS DE CHAILLOT
(Pages 100-103)

UNESCO
Place de Fontenoy (88, O-10). Visits at 11 and 3 daily
This attractive cluster of glass and reinforced concrete buildings was designed for the United Nations Educational, Scientific and Cultural Organization. The buildings are decorated with frescoes by Picasso and Tamayo.

ARCHES AND FOUNTAINS, MONUMENTS AND MEMORIALS

Paris is a city unusually rich in statues, monuments, arches and fountains. On this page are described some of these reminders of the past not covered in detail in Part III of the guide. Monuments of another sort fill the cemeteries. These may make a pilgrimage to the graves of famous men seem like an excursion through a strange open-air museum.

FONTAINE BOUCHARDON
57-59 Rue de Grenelle (26, G-2)
Also known as the Fontaine des Quatre Saisons, this beautiful fountain was built to satisfy 18th Century residents' complaints that their street lacked water; the water no longer flows.

FONTAINE DES INNOCENTS
Square des Innocents (104, G-4)
Domed and magnificently sculptured, this is a Renaissance masterpiece near Les Halles, originally surrounded by a large cemetery. The fountain played for the first time in 1549.

FONTAINE DE L'OBSERVATOIRE
Avenue de l'Observatoire (26, M-10)
In this 19th Century work, four lithe nudes shoulder a huge globe above eight leaping sea horses and porpoises.

HENRI IV
Pont-Neuf (26, N-1)
This favorite Paris landmark has experienced vicissitudes. The original statue fell into the sea en route from Italy. The present statue dates from 1818, when a statue of Napoleon was melted to provide the bronze. Legend has it that a statuette of the emperor was slipped into Henri's right arm by the vengeful Bonapartist sculptor.

JEANNE D'ARC
Place des Pyramides (59, T-7)
A gallant bronze-gilt figure of Joan of Arc on horseback stands a few yards from the spot where Joan fell wounded in an attack on English-occupied Paris (1429). Parisians make a pilgrimage to the statue on May 30, the date of her death.

PORTE ST-DENIS
Boulevard St-Denis (Paris map, front end paper, K-4)
Through this triumphal arch the kings of France rode in their carriages on their ceremonial entrances into Paris. Built in 1672, it honors Louis XIV's victorious campaigns against Holland and Germany. It was, at 79 feet, the highest arch in Paris until the construction of the 164-foot-high Arc de Triomphe. Above the portal is a sculpted figure of the king leading his troops across the Rhine.

PORTE ST-MARTIN
Boulevard St-Martin (Paris map, front end paper, K-4)
Louis XIV, honored in this arch built two years after the Porte St-Denis (*above*), is shown as a naked Hercules leaning on a club.

STATUE OF LIBERTY
Pont de Grenelle (88, D-9)
The U.S. presented this small copy of the Statue of Liberty to France in 1889 in appreciation for the original French gift. The replica stands on a small island in the Seine, the Allée des Cygnes, and can be seen from excursion boats.

CIMETIÈRE MONTMARTRE
20 Avenue Rachel (138, C-2)
The famous men lying here include composer Hector Berlioz and authors Jean Giraudoux and Alexandre Dumas.

CIMETIÈRE MONTPARNASSE
3 Boulevard Edgar-Quinet (26, H-10)
In this 45-acre cemetery are the graves of poet Charles Baudelaire and writer Guy de Maupassant.

CIMETIÈRE DE PASSY
Off Place du Trocadéro (88, F-2) Métro Trocadéro at Paul-Doumer exit
The painter Edouard Manet and the composer Claude Debussy are buried in this small cemetery.

CIMETIÈRE DU PÈRE LACHAISE
Boulevard de Ménilmontant (105, Y-3)
"To be buried in Père Lachaise," said Victor Hugo of Paris' largest cemetery, "is like having mahogany furniture." Elaborate mausoleums and tombstones commemorate Rossini, Colette, Chopin, La Fontaine and Oscar Wilde.

CIMETIÈRE DE PICPUS
35 Rue de Picpus (Paris map, front end paper, N-7) Métro Picpus. Open from 2 p.m. to dark
Lafayette's bones, in soil brought from the U.S., lie among those of victims of the Revolution.

SMALL WONDERS
AND UNUSUAL TOURS

The Paris of magnificent palaces, parks and museums is well known. But Paris is full of secrets and surprises. Many of its most curious and colorful sights are hidden away in back streets, and the strangest of them are literally underground. Each of the places listed below makes an interesting visit and sheds an unfamiliar light on the city's history.

ARÈNES DE LUTÈCE
At the foot of Montagne Ste-Geneviève (27, S-8). Entrance at 10 Rue des Arènes, 49 Rue Monge and Rue Navarre
In the Second and Third Centuries, some 10,000 spectators used to crowd into this Roman arena to watch gladiators in combat. It was also a theater for dramas and comedies. Some of the dressing rooms still stand. It was excavated in the 19th Century.

BIRD MARKET
Place Louis-Lépine, Île de la Cité (26, Q-2). Open 9-6 Sundays only
For generations birds of all kinds have been sold here on Sundays, when they and their keepers take over the area occupied on weekdays by the flower market. The main bird business takes place on the Quai de la Mégisserie.

THE CATACOMBS
2 Place Denfert-Rochereau (Paris map, front end paper, H-9). Open the first and third Saturdays of the month and every Saturday July 1-October 15. The tour begins at 2 p.m.
In quarries dug by the Romans into the hills of Montparnasse, Montsouris and Montrouge lie several million skeletons, moved from overcrowded cemeteries in the 18th and 19th Centuries.

FLEA MARKET
(Pages 148-149)

FLOWER MARKET
Place Louis-Lépine, Île de la Cité (26, Q-2). Open 9-12, 2-6 except Sundays

In this open-air market the sidewalks and stands are a patchwork of vivid colors. The flowers are cheaper than at florists, and strolling through the market is one of Paris' pleasant diversions.

GATEHOUSES OF THE FERMIERS GÉNÉRAUX WALL
At the Rotonde de la Villette (139, S-4); Place Denfert-Rochereau (Paris map, front end paper, H-9); Place de la Nation (Paris map, front end paper, N-7); La Rotonde in the Parc Monceau (126, K-1).
These two pavilions are remnants of 47 tollgates put up by Louis XVI's tax collectors, the Fermiers Généraux.

GOBELINS TAPESTRY WORKS
42 Avenue des Gobelins (Paris map, front end paper, K-9). Open 2-4 Wednesdays, Thursdays and Fridays
The intricate art of handweaving that flourished under the Bourbons has not changed much since the looms were moved here in 1601. Some of the looms that made tapestries for Versailles may still be in operation. Weavers hunched at their racks sometimes spend years on a single piece of work. The industry was once owned by the kings and now by the state. Masterpieces of the past and present are on display.

LES HALLES
(Pages 110-113)

MUSÉE GRÉVIN
10 Boulevard Montmartre (127, X-5). Open 2-7 daily, 2-11 Saturdays, Sundays and holidays
The Continent's oldest wax museum.

THE OLDEST HOUSE IN PARIS
3 Rue Volta (104, K-1)
This four-story dwelling was erected around 1300.

SEWERS
Place de la Concorde, near Statue de Lille (58, Q-6). Open second and fourth Thursdays of May and June, every Thursday July to October 15, the last Saturday of May, June, July and September; tours at 2, 3, 4 and 5 p.m.
The sewers of Paris are quite clean, and a descent into them is fascinating. You can sail on one main tunnel from the Concorde to the Madeleine.

STAMP MARKET
Avenue Gabriel between Avenues Marignan and Matignon (58, M-4). Open all day Thursdays, Saturdays, Sundays, holidays
Here valuable stamps are bought and sold at open-air tables.

TOUR ST-JACQUES
Square St-Jacques (104, G-5)
This tower is a remnant of a church destroyed in the Revolution. Today it is a weather station closed to the public.

A GUIDE TO CHURCHES, GREAT AND SMALL

There are churches by the hundreds in Paris, and in nearly every one there are reverent reminders of the long history of Christianity in France. The selection on these pages ranges from an ancient church containing columns taken from Roman temples to classical and 19th Century buildings. Nearly all are open weekdays as well as Sundays.

NOTRE-DAME DE PARIS
(Pages 32-37)

Churches on the Right Bank

ST-EUSTACHE
2 Rue du Jour (104, E-2)
The church stands next to Les Halles; a soaring Gothicism and the sculptured Renaissance *décor* give it a beauty second only to Notre-Dame. Over 100 feet above the floor the richly ornamented vaults branch into a maze of ribbing. The church was completed by 1637.
• *Highlights:* organ music and choristers, Sundays at 11; Jean Baptiste Pigalle's statue of the Virgin.

ST-GERMAIN L'AUXERROIS
2 Place du Louvre (59, X-10)
In this parish church of the Louvre palace generations of French royalty worshiped. Over centuries they added to its conglomerate architectural style. A fine collection of religious objects belonging to the royal families completes this museum of royal tastes.
• *Highlights:* a peaked porch, one of the best Gothic structures in Paris; 17th Century church-warden's pew.

ST-GERVAIS-ST-PROTAIS
2 Rue François-Miron (104, J-7)
The contrast between the severe neoclassical facade and the late-Gothic flamboyant style of the rest of this church reveals the old French flair for

SAINTE-CHAPELLE
(Pages 40-43)

incongruity. On Good Friday in 1918 a German Big Bertha shell killed 50 worshipers here.
• *Highlights:* the ornate tomb of Louis XIV's chancellor, Michel Le Tellier; the oldest organ in Paris.

THE MADELEINE
(Pages 128-129)

ST-PAUL-ST-LOUIS
99 Rue St-Antoine (104, M-7)
A Jesuit version of the 17th Century baroque was launched here and Jesuit orators reached their brilliant peak preaching from its pulpit. For almost a century the royal court and much of the aristocracy came to hear the intellectual sermons—often three hours long. The Jesuit order was banished from France amid religious controversies in 1762.

ST-PIERRE DE MONTMARTRE
2 Rue du Mont-Cenis (138, H-2)
An extremely ancient church, St-Pierre

Churches on the Left Bank

DÔME DES INVALIDES
(Pages 94-95)

ST-ÉTIENNE DU MONT
Place Ste-Geneviève (26, Q-7)
Begun in 1492 to replace a smaller church, St-Étienne du Mont is a graceful blend of Gothic design and Renais-

was restored at the turn of this century and is considered the most likable structure on the hill. An early 12th Century Gothic exterior complements the simple, well-lit interior in which stand four columns of Roman times. The first Christians of Paris probably worshiped around here; both a Sixth Century basilica and an older Roman temple stood on the hill.

ST-ROCH
296 Rue St-Honoré (59, T-6)
This church, built between 1653 and 1740 in the Jesuit baroque style, is one of the longest in Paris. Bullet marks on the outside walls of this church date from 1795, when Napoleon, then a youthful revolutionary officer, put down a royalist uprising. A collection of 17th and 18th Century sculpture and painting is outstanding.

BASILIQUE DU SACRÉ-COEUR
(Pages 146-147)

sance decoration, with some lovely stained glass windows made between 1550 and 1600. The exquisite Renaissance choir screen is the only one of its kind left in Paris.
• *Highlight:* Ste-Geneviève's chapel, which contains the only fragment from the tomb of Paris' patron saint.

ST-GERMAIN DES PRÉS

3 Place St-Germain-des-Prés (26, K-2)
The best view of this, the oldest Parisian church, is from the side terrace of the Café des Deux Magots. The Romanesque bell tower, dating from 1014, is the oldest part of St-Germain. Inside, the Romanesque nave and early Gothic choir form an interesting combination of the two styles. Portions of the interior columns stood in the original Sixth Century chapel on whose remains St-Germain was built.
• *Highlight:* the large 19th Century murals, dramatizing tales from the Old and New Testaments.

ST-JULIEN-LE-PAUVRE

1 Rue St-Julien-le-Pauvre (27, Q-3)
St-Julien-le-Pauvre is a combination of Romanesque and early Gothic architecture. Built in the 12th and 13th Centuries, it is picturesque for its very lack of architectural pretension. It is now a Greek Catholic church.
• *Highlights:* one of the best views of Notre Dame here; a quiet garden that shelters it from the 20th Century.

ST-LOUIS DES INVALIDES

Esplanade des Invalides (88, R-7)
Some of France's famous generals, including General Leclerc, a leader of the Free French in World War II, are interred here close by the Église du Dôme (tomb of Napoleon). Captured enemy standards are hung from the walls.
• *Highlights:* Napoleon's death mask and the copper coffin used to carry his body from St. Helena to Paris in 1840, in the Chapelle Napoléon.

ST-SÉVERIN

1 Rue des Prêtres—St-Séverin (26, P-3)
For nearly 1,500 years people have worshiped where St-Séverin stands; the first of several churches on the site was burned by the Normans. Inside, rugged early Gothic styles compete with the complicated flamboyance of the 15th and 16th Centuries.
• *Highlights:* stained glass windows dating from the 14th Century; clock which tolled the curfew for university students during the Middle Ages.

ÉGLISE DE LA SORBONNE

Place de la Sorbonne (26, O-6)
The church is the only one of the university structures built under Cardinal Richelieu's original plan that remains unaltered. The church serves as the university chapel, and for a long time Richelieu's descendants were the only people who enjoyed the privilege of being married and buried there.
• *Highlights:* Richelieu's tomb, a masterpiece of the 17th Century sculptor François Girardon, showing Richelieu on his deathbed; above it hangs the Cardinal's red hat.

ST-SULPICE

Place St-Sulpice (26, L-4)
This is the second largest church in Paris. Its classic columns illustrate the ancient Doric, Ionic and Corinthian styles. One of the two towers at the front of the church is unfinished because funds ran out at the end of 134 years of construction (1646-1780).
• *Highlights:* the 19th Century murals by Delacroix, some of his finest work; the organ, considered to be the best in France, played on Sundays at 11:30.

VAL-DE-GRÂCE

Place Alphonse-Laveran (26, N-10)
Queen Anne, barren during 23 years of marriage, built this church in gratitude for the birth of an heir. The heir became Louis XIV in 1643, at the age of five. When he was seven he laid the cornerstone of this baroque church. One of the architects, Le Duc, inspired by a stay in Rome, created an elaborate dome and a high altar that resemble those of St. Peter's in Rome.
• *Highlight: The Glory of the Blessed* by Pierre Mignard, a vast composition inside the dome, with 200 figures three times life size.

Churches with Religious Services in English

Protestant
AMERICAN CATHEDRAL
23 Avenue George-V

AMERICAN CHURCH
65 Quai d'Orsay

BAPTIST 48 Rue de Lille

MORMON 3 Rue Lota

CHRISTIAN SCIENCE
10 Avenue d'Iéna

METHODIST 4 Rue Roquépine

PRESBYTERIAN
17 Rue Bayard

QUAKER 110 Avenue Mozart

Catholic
ST. JOSEPH'S CHURCH
50 Avenue Hoche

Jewish
GREAT SYNAGOGUE
44 Rue de la Victoire

LIBERAL SYNAGOGUE
24 Rue Copernic

Number and letter combinations in parentheses are map references; i.e., "(127, T-5)" means page 127, location T-5.

RACES TO WATCH
AND SPORTS TO PLAY

Horse racing in Paris is at its most beautiful. But Paris also offers many participant sports; some are listed below. It's wise to phone for particulars.

Swimming, Tennis, Golf and Riding

PISCINE DELIGNY
Opposite 25 Quai Anatole-France (89, U-2) INV 72-15
Pool on the Seine. Open May 1-September 30. Admission: 3.50 NF.

PISCINE AT THE HOTEL CLARIDGE
74 Avenue des Champs-Élysées (58, J-3) ELY 33-01
Indoor pool, public admitted. Open daily. Admission: 5.50 NF.

PISCINE MOLITOR
1 Avenue de la Porte-Molitor (150, D-9) AUT 91-49; *outdoor pool, 8 Avenue de la Porte-Molitor,* BAG 76-92
Admission: indoor pool 1.80 NF, outdoor, in summer 3.50 NF.

TENNIS
Tennis is difficult to arrange in Paris. Call the Fédération Française de Lawn-Tennis, 3 Rue Volney, OPE 44-91.

GOLF
Some golf clubs will let you play, but your best chances are on weekdays. The two nearest to Paris are the Golf de St-Cloud, 6 miles (*Environs map, front end paper, G-6*) Tel. 926-22-83, and Golf St-Germain-en-Laye, 15 miles (*Environs map, front end paper, G-6*) Tel. 963-05-90. The Fédération Française de Golf, 9 Rue de Miromesnil (*126, N-5*) ANJ 26-43, can be of help.

LE MANÈGE MONTEVIDEO
7 Rue de Montevideo (150, Q-10) TRO 33-63
10 NF per hour for a riding lesson, 12 NF for a group ride.

MANÈGE LICART
21 Rue de la Ferme, Neuilly-sur-Seine (150, R-4) MAI 81-86
11 NF per hour for a riding lesson, 13.20 NF for a group ride.

Horse Racing

AUTEUIL
Bois de Boulogne (150, H-9) ELY 33-80
Steeplechase races from mid-February through April, end of May to mid-July, October to mid-December. Important events: Prix du Président de la République (Easter Sunday), Grand Steeplechase de Paris (the next-to-last Sunday in June), Grande Course des Haies (Wednesday before the last Sunday in June).

CHANTILLY
Chantilly, 25 miles from Paris (Environs map, front end paper, J-3) ELY 96-25
Flat races June, July, September. Important events: Prix de Diane (first Sunday in June), Prix du Jockey Club (second Sunday in June).

ENGHIEN
Enghien, 7 miles from Paris (Environs map, front end paper, H-5) ELY 20-70
Steeplechase and trotting mid-February to December. Main events: Grand Steeplechase d'Enghien (first Monday in October), International Meeting of Trotting (early August).

LONGCHAMP
Bois de Boulogne (150, H-2) ELY 96-25
Probably the most beautiful course in the world. The flat racing season has a full schedule that lasts from April to October. Major events include: Grand Prix de Paris (last Sunday in June), Prix de l'Arc de Triomphe (first or second Sunday in October).

MAISONS-LAFFITTE
9 miles from Paris (Environs map, front end paper, G-5) ELY 20-70
The flat racing season continues from March to November. Important events: Prix Robert Papin (last Sunday in July), La Coupe de Maisons-Laffitte (September).

ST-CLOUD
Route du Camp Canadien (Environs map, front end paper, G-6) ELY 20-70
The flat racing season lasts from March to December. Major events: Grand Prix de St-Cloud (first Sunday in July), Prix Eugène Adam (third Sunday in July).

VINCENNES
Bois de Vincennes (Environs map, front end paper, J-6) ENT 55-44
Trotting races last from mid-August to mid-September, mid-November to the end of February. Evening races April-July. Events of importance: Prix du Président de la République (June), Grand Prix d'Été (September), Prix d'Amérique (January).

THE IDYLLIC LIFE
IN MANY PARKS

The parks of Paris are the bud that causes the whole city to flower. Many are but a bright touch in a neighborhood. Others, like those listed below, are virtual Edens of pleasure.

Right Bank

BOIS DE BOULOGNE
(Pages 152-155)

JARDIN D'ACCLIMATATION
In the Bois de Boulogne, near the Porte Maillot (151, S-6)
There is no better way of amusing children than by taking them here. A miniature train conducts you from the Porte Maillot to the garden's entrance. The slides and sand pits may keep the young so busy that the huge floral clock seems to race along. Gay balloons, a small zoo and a bowling alley will round out a child's delight.
• *Highlight:* an exotic ride at the zoo in a cart pulled by an ostrich.

PARC DES BUTTES-CHAUMONT
Between Rues Manin, de Crimée and Botzaris (139, Y-6)
The 60-acre park at Buttes-Chaumont was a wasteland of unused quarries and a rubbish dump before Haussmann landscaped it in one of his great triumphs of city planning. Families from its grim working class environs picnic on its lawns and hillsides. Men play chess under chestnut trees, pompadoured sailors take their girl friends boating on a lake, and children are everywhere. Maurice Chevalier, living nearby as a boy, had his first glimpses of gaiety on its malls and in its cafés.
• *Highlight:* from an imitation Roman temple on the island in the lake, a magnificent view of Sacré Coeur and Montmartre.

PARC MONCEAU
Rue de Monceau and Boulevard de Courcelles (126, K-1)
Well-born children are in charge here, and they lead a charmed life that will charm you. These 23 acres which belonged to Louis-Philippe were bought by the city and redesigned by Haussmann, but they remain largely a preserve of the wealthy who live around the park. Watched by English nannies, little girls still run through gardens wearing white gloves, and very young gentlemen in flannels tricycle about.
• *Highlight:* a curved colonnade at the edge of the beautiful pond.

Left Bank

CHAMP-DE-MARS
Behind the Eiffel Tower (88, L-6)
Originally a parade ground for the nearby École Militaire, the Champ-de-Mars has seen as much disorder as drill since it was laid out in the 18th Century. Revolutionary riots and five world fairs (1867, 1878, 1889, 1900, 1937) all occurred on the 1,000-yard-long green leading to the banks of the Seine. Nowadays platoons of baby carriages have replaced the marching cadets.
• *Highlight:* a close-up view of the Eiffel Tower.

JARDIN DU LUXEMBOURG
(Pages 54-55)

JARDIN DES PLANTES
Place Valhubert (27, U-9)
Since the public was first admitted, generations of Parisians have been enjoying the ever-increasing collection of exotic flora brought from all over the world. It was named the Muséum National d'Histoire Naturelle in 1793. The garden also boasts the "Robinier," the oldest tree in Paris, planted by the botanist Robin in 1601.
• *Highlight:* a zoo which once housed beasts from the king's menagerie.

PARC DE MONTSOURIS
Avenue du Parc de Montsouris (Paris map, front end paper, H-10)
Montsouris, which means "the hill of mice," earned its name when the area was covered with grain mills, a rodent's paradise. The 39 acres are now a favorite of students from the nearby Cité Universitaire. There is a pleasant restaurant by a lake and a small palace used in the Exposition of 1867.

JARDIN DES TUILERIES
(Pages 76-77)

JARDIN DU MUSÉE RODIN
77 Rue de Varenne (89, S-6)
The old garden where 18th Century aristocrats used to sip tea has been taken over by a collection of Rodin's sculpture. For a background, there are some of the most beautiful trees in Paris and 1,000 species of roses.
• *Highlights:* Rodin's *The Thinker*, *The Kiss* and the *Burghers of Calais*.

Number and letter combinations in parentheses are map references; i.e., "(127, T-5)" means page 127, location T-5.

EXCURSIONS TO TAKE
IN THE PARIS REGION

Paris is surrounded by a belt of forests and valleys 60 miles wide studded with cathedrals and castles. Here the Sun King ruled, there Napoleon bade farewell to his troops and everywhere are wonders worth exploring by guided tour (check travel agencies) or on your own. To locate the sites described, see the footnote on the opposite page.

Southwest of Paris

VERSAILLES

Located 13 miles west of Paris, Versailles (G-6) is reached by automobile via Porte de St-Cloud and the superhighway Autoroute de l'Ouest; by train from the Gare St-Lazare. The palace is open from 10 to 5 except Tuesdays; the gardens from 9 to 6.
The most magnificently boastful monument in all France is the palace at Versailles. Here in 1783 England signed the armistice that conceded victory to its former colonies in America; here in 1871 the German conquerors of Paris proclaimed the Prussian king Emperor of Germany. But mainly this palace speaks of French history. It was, after 1682, the seat of government of its builder, Louis XIV, who carried the white banners of the Bourbon kings to

their crest of glory, and of Louis XV, who frittered it all away, and of the ill-fated Louis XVI, who watched helplessly as the monarchy collapsed. A visit to the Great Apartments of State can be managed in an hour. But it takes the better part of a day really to explore the palace and wander through the gardens to the pleasant places where kings took their ease: the Petit Trianon, Grand Trianon and "Little Village" where Marie Antoinette pretended she was just a peasant girl.
• *Highlight:* worthy of a visit in any season, Versailles is probably at its best on the first or third Sunday evening of any month from May to October. That is when its leaping fountains are illuminated and played.

CHARTRES

Located 60 miles from Paris, Chartres (C-10) is reached by automobile via the Autoroute de l'Ouest, direction Rambouillet, then Route Nationale 10; by train from the Gare Montparnasse. Services before 10; open to visitors after 10.
The great soaring cathedral of Notre-Dame de Chartres that dominates the flat wheat country west of Paris is the essence of a France whose faith was undivided. It was constructed during the 12th Century in a great national outburst of religious fervor that fol-

lowed the Crusades. The result is one of civilization's treasures. There are two asymmetrical towers and between them a facade that is one of the most famous pieces of religious sculpture in France; it tells the story of Christ's life and also shows a number of Biblical kings and queens with expressive faces.
• *Highlights:* the celebrated stained glass windows, glowing with the special "Chartres blue" and dating from the 12th and 13th Centuries; the winding maze through which pilgrims moved on their knees.

Southeast of Paris

VINCENNES

Located 7 miles from Paris, the Château de Vincennes (J-6) is reached by Métro (Château de Vincennes station); for the zoo, go to the Porte Dorée or Porte de Charenton station. The château is open 10-12, 1:30-5 (6 in summer) every day except Tuesdays and holidays, with guided tours at 10, 11, 1:30, 2:30, 3:30, 4:30 (and 5:30 in summer). The zoo is open 9-7 daily April 1-September 30, 9-6 in winter.
The rectangular royal stronghold in the Bois de Vincennes has played an important role in French history since the 13th Century when King Louis IX (St-Louis) dispensed justice while sitting under an oak tree here. England's King Henry V died of dysentery in it in 1422. French governments have used

it as a prison; Napoleon had the Duc d'Enghien shot here. The castle contains mementos of all these people. Nearby is the Vincennes zoo, one of the finest in Europe, and the great Bois de Vincennes.

FONTAINEBLEAU

Located 38 miles from Paris, Fontainebleau (K-10) is reached by auto via the Porte d'Italie, the superhighway Autoroute de Sud and Route Nationale 7; by train from the Gare de Lyon. The château is open 10-12, 1:15-4 October 1-March 31, till 5 the rest of year.
The Renaissance palace at Fontainebleau is famed for a feminine elegance —and to many of the kings of France it was closely associated with charming

women. François I built it for his mistress, the Duchesse d'Étampes. Henri II added to it for his mistress, Diane de Poitiers. Henri IV enlarged it for his mistress, Gabrielle d'Estrées, and Louis XIV further improved it while he was carrying on a love affair here with Louise de la Vallière.

West of Paris

MALMAISON

Located 10 miles from Paris, Malmaison (G-6) is reached by car from the Porte Maillot via Route Nationale 13; by train from the Gare St-Lazare. The château is open 10:30-12, 1:30-4:30 (5:30 in summer) except Tuesdays and holidays.

The château at Malmaison is a memorial to Napoleon Bonaparte's first wife, Josephine Tascher de la Pagerie. She was a gay and lovely lady with expensive tastes. When Napoleon divorced her he settled 3.6 million francs on her and two years later she was 1.2 million francs in debt. The elaborate gardens and beautiful furniture and jewels and paintings exhibited at Malmaison show where the money went.

North and Northeast of Paris

ST-DENIS

Located 7 miles from Paris, St-Denis (H-5) is reached by car via the Porte de la Chapelle and Route Nationale 1; by train from the Gare du Nord.

Since the days of Dagobert I (ending in 638) the kings of France have been interred in the Basilica at St-Denis. Here, too, Pepin the Short divided his

ST-GERMAIN-EN-LAYE

Located 15 miles from Paris, St-Germain-en-Laye (F-6) is reached by car via the Porte Maillot and Route Nationale 13; by train from the Gare St-Lazare. The château is open 10-12, 1:30-5 except Tuesdays and holidays.

Constructed on the edge of a plateau with a panoramic view, the Royal Palace at St-Germain-en-Laye was a favorite retreat for French kings when the Paris mobs were on the march. There is a lovely Gothic chapel built by Louis IX in 1230 and a great hall—the Salle de Mars—scene of Louis XIV's spectacular entertainments.
• *Highlight:* charming chapel, a gem of Gothic architecture.

realm between his sons, Charlemagne and Carloman, and here Abélard, separated from his dear Héloise, remained. Ste-Jeanne d'Arc hung up her arms in this church hoping to fight no more, and Henri IV in pomp abjured his Protestantism here. The church, dedicated to St-Denis, who legend says walked here after his head was cut off on Montmartre, is full of statues and empty tombs of kings, queens, noble princes and illustrious persons dating from the Seventh Century (the bodies were flung into a common grave during the Revolution).
• *Highlight:* In a crypt under the church are statues and coffins of Louis XVI and Marie Antoinette, who came to share St-Denis' notable lack of a head.

CHANTILLY

Located 25 miles from Paris, Chantilly (J-3) is reached by auto via the Porte de la Chapelle, Route Nationale 1 to St-Denis and 16 to Chantilly; by train from the Gare du Nord. The Grand Château and the Petit Château are open from the first Sunday in March through October, 1:30-5:30 (to 6 May-September); Sundays 10-6; closed Tuesdays and race days (for races see page 194). The Great Stables are open 2-5 Thursdays and Sundays from Easter to November 1, except on race days.

Chantilly is famous for whipped cream, lace, horse racing and an estate containing two châteaux and a huge 18th Century stable for 250 horses and 400 dogs. In the Petit Château (Châtelet), built in the 16th Century for a warrior duke of Montmorency, are elaborate woodwork and painted panels. The Grand Château houses the art treasures of the Condé family. They include Italian paintings by Perugino, Raphael and Titian; French paintings by Poussin, Ingres and Corot; and the *Très Riches Heures du Duc de Berri* by the Limbourg brothers and the *Heures d'Étienne Chevalier* by Jean Fouquet, two of the finest examples of medieval illuminated manuscripts in the world.
• *Highlight:* on display on Sundays only, the Grand Condé, a huge rose diamond stolen and recovered in 1926.

COMPIÈGNE

Located 47 miles from Paris, Compiègne (L-1) is reached by car via Porte de la Villette, Routes Nationales 2, 17 and 32; by train from the Gare du Nord. The château is open 10-12, 2-5 March through October; 10-12, 2-4:30 the rest of the year except November 1, December 25, January 1.

Under Compiègne's walls Jeanne d'Arc was captured and started on her journey to the stake in Rouen market place. The castle was the scene of many gay parties during the reign of Napoleon III. It now contains a fine 18th Century furniture display and a fascinating museum of land transport.
• *Highlight:* Parked on a siding in the woods nearby is a replica of the railroad coach in which the Germans on November 11, 1918, signed the armistice ending World War I; in the same railroad coach, on June 22, 1940, the French signed the armistice ending the Battle of France.

Number and letter combinations in parentheses refer to locations on the Environs map found on the front end paper.

CREDITS

The sources for the illustrations in this book are shown below. Credits for pictures from left to right are separated by commas, top to bottom by dashes.

Cover: Simon Nathan from Nancy Palmer Agency. End-paper maps by Lothar Roth. 5: Brassaï from Rapho-Guillumette. 6, 7: Drawings by Charlotte Winter. 10: Herbert Orth courtesy The Philadelphia Museum of Art, Éditions du Pont Royal. 11: Wide World Photos, Man Ray Collection, Culver Pictures–Éditions du Pont Royal–Wide World Photos. 16, 17: Pierre Boulat. 18 through 21: Drawings by Martha Blake. 24 through 27: Maps by Lothar Roth. 28, 29: Pierre Belzeaux from Rapho-Guillumette. 30, 31: Drawing by Charlotte Winter. 32, 33: Charles E. Rotkin from Photography for Industry, drawing by Joseph Bertelli. 34, 35: Drawings by Martha Blake. 36: Henri Cartier-Bresson from Magnum. 37: Cultural History Research, Inc., Harrison, New York. 38, 39: Bernard G. Silberstein from Rapho-Guillumette, drawing by Martha Blake, Pierre Boulat, Leslie Gill courtesy The Phillips Collection, Washington, D.C. 40: Pierre Boulat. 41: Drawing by Martha Blake, Frédérique Duran. 42, 43: Frédérique Duran. 44: Pierre Boulat. 45: Cultural History Research, Inc. courtesy Bibliothèque Nationale. 47: Map by Joseph Bertelli. 48: Pierre Boulat. 49: J. E. Bulloz. 50: Jules Aarons from Gamma, Pierre Boulat. 51: Pierre Boulat–Jean Marquis for TIME. 53: Map by Joseph Bertelli. 54: Willy Ronis, Pierre Boulat. 55: E. Boubat from Réalités, Willy Ronis. 56, 57: M. J. Dain. 58, 59: Map by Lothar Roth. 60, 61: Charles E. Rotkin for Photography for Industry. 62: Drawing by Martha Blake. 63: Giraudon (2), Bulloz (2). 64: Bulloz, Dominique Lajoux from Rapho-Guillumette, Bulloz. 65: Taurgo, Bulloz, Giraudon. 66: Drawing by Martha Blake. 67: Fernand Bourges, Bulloz, Camera Clix. 68: Giraudon, Camera Clix, Bulloz. 69: Camera Clix; except left Dominique Lajoux from Rapho-Guillumette. 70: Camera Clix, Fernand Bourges, Peter Adelberg from European Art Color Slide Co. 71: Cultural History Research, Inc.; except left Larry Burrows for TIME. 72: Giraudon, Eric Schaal. 73: Cultural History Research, Inc.; except left Delacroix from Camera Clix. 74: Cultural History Research, Inc., Giraudon. 75: Drawing by Martha Blake–Cultural History Research, Inc., Les Archives Photographiques d'Art et d'Histoire, Giraudon. 76: Frank Horvat from Magnum, Ken Heyman from Rapho-Guillumette. 77: Ken Heyman from Rapho-Guillumette; except left Refot from Rapho-Guillumette. 78: Drawing by Robert Riley–collection of Jeanne de Lanux. 79: John Bryson. 80, 81: Pierre Boulat. 82, 83: Left Charles May from Monkmeyer Press Photo Service; center Ed Van der Elsken from Rapho-Guillumette; right Robert Doisneau from Rapho-Guillumette–Jean Mounicq from Pix. 84: Pierre Boulat. 85: French Cultural Services; except right Jean Marquis for TIME. 86, 87: Charles E. Rotkin from Photography for Industry, drawing by Joseph Bertelli, Alliance Gaston from Black Star. 88, 89: Map by Lothar Roth. 90: Anthony Linck. 91: Drawing by Martha Blake, Pierre Boulat. 92: Charles E. Rotkin from Photography for Industry, Loomis Dean courtesy Musée de l'Armée, Invalides, Paris. 93: S.P.A.D.E.M. courtesy Musée de l'Armée, Invalides, Paris; except right Michel Brodsky. 94, 95: Eddy Van der Veen courtesy Archives Nationales–Charles E. Rotkin from Photography for Industry. 96, 97: Photos Chevojon; except top left Wide World Photos. 98, 99: Charles Ciccione from Rapho-Guillumette. 100: Drawing by Martha Blake–Jean Marquis. 101: Musée de la Marine; except left Jean Marquis. 102: Dmitri Kessel. 103: Collection Musée de l'Homme-José Oster; except center Collection Musée de l'Homme. 104, 105: Map by Lothar Roth. 106, 107: Robert Doisneau from Rapho-Guillumette, Sanford H. Roth from Rapho-Guillumette. 108, 109: Giraudon, Frank J. Scherschel. 110, 111: Pierre Boulat. 112: Georges Viollon from Gamma, Lies Wiegman from Gamma–Pierre Boulat. 113: Thomas D. McAvoy, Pierre Boulat. 114, 115: Courtesy Bibliothèque Nationale, Paris; Yale Joel, Robert Capa from Magnum. 116: R. Henrard. 117: Courtesy Bibliothèque Nationale, Paris. 119: Map by Joseph Bertelli. 120, 121: L'Arrestation de M. de Launay by Prieur after Berthault Men and Women of the French Revolution by Phillip Gibbs, Philadelphia, Lippincott, 1906. New York Public Library (Werner Wolff, Black Star)–N. R. Farbman. 122: Cultural History Research, Inc. courtesy Musée Carnavalet. 123: Cultural History Research, Inc. courtesy Bibliothèque Nationale, Paris. 124: Cultural History Research, Inc. courtesy Musée de Versailles and Réunion des Musées Internationaux, Culver Pictures. 125: Cultural History Research, Inc. courtesy Musée Carnavalet. 126, 127: Map by Lothar Roth. 128: Willy Ronis. 129: Simon Nathan from Nancy Palmer Agency; except top right Willy Ronis. 130: Pierre Boulat. 131: Cultural History Research, Inc. courtesy Musée Carnavalet, Willy Ronis. 132, 133: Studio Josse Lalance & Co. courtesy Musée Carnavalet. 134: Sergio Larrain from Magnum. 135: Bottom left Sergio Larrain from Magnum; right Pierre Boulat. 136: Sergio Larrain from Magnum. 137: Sergio Larrain from Magnum; except right Brassaï from Rapho-Guillumette for SPORTS ILLUSTRATED. 138, 139: Map by Lothar Roth. 140: Zalewski from Rapho-Guillumette. 141: David Zingg. 142: Perls Galleries–Pierre Boulat. 143: Giraudon, Pierre Boulat. 144: Photo Cauvin, Pierre Boulat, Giraudon. 145: Pierre Boulat; except top right Giraudon. 146, 147: Charles E. Rotkin from Photography for Industry. 148: Pierre Boulat. 149: Robert Riley, Robert Doisneau from Rapho-Guillumette. 150, 151: Lothar Roth. 152: Willy Ronis. 153: Robert Doisneau from Rapho-Guillumette. 154, 155: Pierre Boulat; except center Willy Rizzo from Paris-Match.

ACKNOWLEDGMENTS

The editors are particularly indebted to Henri M. Peyre, Chairman, Department of Romance Languages, Yale University, who served as Chief Consultant; to Page d'Aulnay, Louise Sheldon and Patricia Kusana-Rogereau, who provided editorial assistance in Paris; and to the following members of the TIME-LIFE Paris Bureau: Susie Marquis, Lucy Lane Kelly and James J. De Bovet. Aid was also received from the State Ministry of Cultural Affairs, Paris; Myron Clement, Director of Public Relations, and Angèle Lévesque, Director of the Information Center, French Government Tourist Office, New York; Daisey Lebel of the French Cultural Services of the French Embassy; David Finch of the French Institute, New York; Dr. Claus Virch, Assistant Curator of the European Painting Department, and Dr. Thomas P. F. Hoving, Assistant Curator of the Medieval Art Department, the Metropolitan Museum of Art, New York; Ena Yonge, Map Curator, American Geographical Society; Musée du Louvre, Paris; Horace Sutton; Jeanne de Lanux.

INDEX

This index is arranged in the customary alphabetical order with these exceptions: the names of individual HOTELS, RESTAURANTS, BARS, CAFES, SNACK BARS and NIGHT SPOTS are listed in alphabetical order under their main subject headings (e.g., Le Grand Vefour may be found by looking under RESTAURANTS). In general, French names are alphabetized by the first principal word in the name rather than by the articles, *le* or *la*. For shopping information look under general categories such as JEWELRY, ANTIQUES, etc., rather than under specific shop names. An asterisk (*) indicates an illustration of the subject.

For an explanation of this indexing system see the introductory note on page 199.

Production staff for Time Incorporated
Arthur R. Murphy (Vice President and Director of Production)
Robert E. Foy, James P. Menton and Caroline Ferri
Text photocomposed on Photon equipment
under the direction of Albert J. Dunn and Arthur J. Dunn

Printed by Livermore and Knight Co., Providence, Rhode Island
Bound by R. R. Donnelley & Sons Company, Crawfordsville, Indiana
Paper by The Mead Corporation, Dayton, Ohio

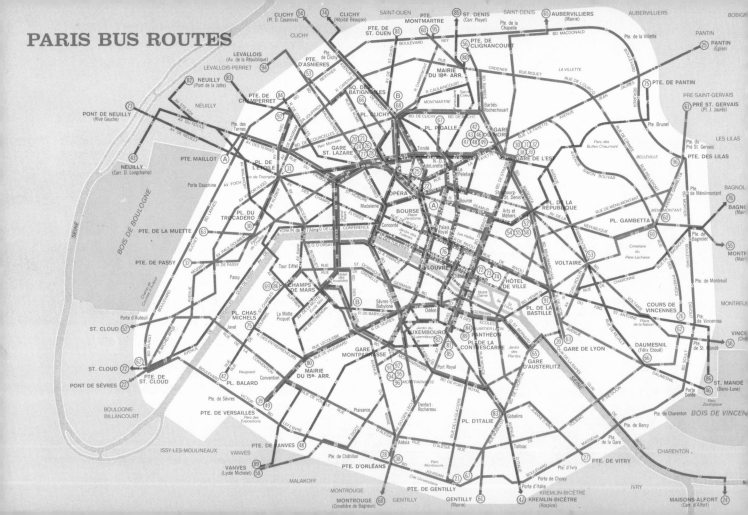

PARIS BUS ROUTES